THE New BELIEVER'S GROWTH BOOK

GREG LAURIE

WORD PUBLISHING

Dallas·London·Vancouver·Melbourne

THE NEW BELIEVER'S GROWTH BOOK

Unless otherwise indicated, Scripture quotations used in this book are from the New King James Version. Copyright ©1979, 1980, 1982, Thomas Nelson, Inc., Publishers.

Those indicated NIV are from the Holy Bible, New International Version of the Bible, copyright ©1973, 1978, 1984 by the New York International Bible Society. Used by permission of Zondervan Bible Publishers.

Those indicated PHILLIPS are from J. B. Phillips: The New Testament in Modern English. Revised Edition. Copyright © J. B. Phillips, 1958, 1960, 1972. Used by permission of Macmillan Publishing Co., Inc.

Those indicated AMP are from The Amplified New Testament. Copyright ©1958 by the Lockman Foundation (used by permission).

Those indicated WUEST'S are from The New Testament: An Expanded Translation by Kenneth S. Wuest. © Copyright Wm. B. Eerdmans Publishing Co. 1961. All rights reserved.

Design: David Riley+Associates, Corona Del Mar, California

ISBN 0-8499-3587-3

Printed in the United States of America

5 6 7 8 9 LB 9 8 7 6 5 4 3

Welcome to God's family!

You may be reading this book because you have made a recent decision to follow Jesus Christ as your Lord and Savior. If so, congratulations, and welcome to the family of God. You have made the most important decision of your life, and I assure you, on the authority of God's Word, you will never regret what you have done. In fact, your only regret will likely be that you did not do this sooner.

Or, you may be reading this book because you want to know more about who Jesus Christ is and what it means to follow Him. Perhaps you have not yet personally asked Him to forgive you of your sins and come into your life. You may even wonder why such a

4

step is necessary. You may think you are already a Christian because other family members are, or because you believe a person named Jesus once walked this earth. You may even think you are going to heaven since you attend church occasionally (or even regularly), or because you try to follow the Ten Commandments. But it is important to know that none of these things in and of themselves necessarily means that you are a Christian!

You are not born a Christian. As Jesus declared, "You must be born again." What does that mean? Let's find out together. I hope this book will help you discover what it means to take that vital step.

Greg Laurie

5

Born Again!

? *Have you ever wondered why you are here on this earth?*

? *What your purpose is in life?*

? *And what happens after death?*

The answers to these and countless other questions are found in the message of the gospel. But what is the gospel? The word "gospel" means "good news," and that's exactly what it is. Before we can fully appreciate that good news, however, we need to first know the bad news. The bad news is that we are separated from God by something called sin.

Many bristle at such an idea, thinking they are not sinners. Yet the Bible clearly tells us that "all have sinned and fall short of the glory of God" (Rom. 3:23) and, "There is none righteous, no, not one" (Rom. 3:10).

One definition of the word sin is "to miss the mark." God is holy and absolutely perfect. He has told us to "be perfect, just as your Father in heaven is perfect" (Matt. 5:48). Of course, none of us could ever come close to doing that—even on our best days! We have all clearly "missed the mark."

Someone might argue, "This isn't fair! I haven't broken as many of the laws of God as some others have!" Yet the Bible tells us, "For whoever shall keep the whole law, and yet stumble in one point, he is guilty of all" (James 2:10). In other words, one sin is enough to keep you separated from God!

This is the most serious of penalties. The Bible tells us that "the wages of sin is death" (Rom. 6:23) and, "The soul who sins shall die" (Eze. 18:20).

THE GAP

So how do you answer to the questions posed at the beginning of this section: "Why am I here on this earth? What is my purpose in life?" The answer is that God created you in His image so that you could know Him in a personal way and discover the unique plan He has "custom made" for your life.

When we don't have this relationship with God, we experience a void and emptiness in our lives. Many try to fill this void with relationships with people. Others try to fill it with success in a career or by acquiring possessions. Some try to fill it with the pursuit of pleasure. Still others try to live moral lives and even seek to fill their lives with religion. Yet even that won't do it.

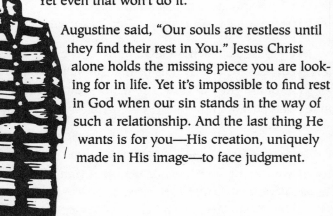

Augustine said, "Our souls are restless until they find their rest in You." Jesus Christ alone holds the missing piece you are looking for in life. Yet it's impossible to find rest in God when our sin stands in the way of such a relationship. And the last thing He wants is for you—His creation, uniquely made in His image—to face judgment.

8

THE SOLUTION

God is keenly aware of our inability to reach Him on our own. He is also aware of how impossible it is for us to meet His standards on even our best days. Thus, He took drastic measures and reached out to us by sending His Son, Jesus Christ, to this earth.

Jesus is probably the most admired man in human history. Many see Him as a great prophet, a model humanitarian, and the ultimate teacher. But He was much more than just a good man: He was the "God-man." Jesus was fully God and fully man. He never sinned when He walked this earth, yet He was exposed to the pressures and difficulties we all face in life. And He willingly went to a Roman cross and died for our sin. With one hand Jesus took hold of a Holy God; with the other He took hold of sinful man. Nails were then driven through those hands, and Jesus became that bridge to the God from whom we are all separated.

9

I once read the story of a judge who was known for the particularly harsh sentences he handed down in his courtroom. One day his own son was arrested for a crime. When the day of sentencing came, the courtroom was packed with people curious to see if the judge would be as harsh with his son as he had been with others. Much to the surprise of those in attendance, the judge gave his son the harshest sentence with the stiffest fine possible under the law. An audible gasp was heard when the verdict was read. Then, without explanation, the judge took off his judicial robes, laid down his gavel, and descended from his bench. Standing next to his son, he announced, "As a judge, I have executed the law, but as this boy's father, I will personally pay the fine."

This is what God did at the Cross. As a Righteous Judge, His demands had to be met; but as our Loving Father, He personally paid the price for our sins. Jesus said, "For God so loved the world that He gave His only begotten Son, that whoever believes in Him should not perish but have everlasting life" (John 3:16). The Bible also tells us, "But God demonstrates His own love toward us, in that while we were still sinners, Christ died for us" (Rom. 5:8).

THE BALL'S IN YOUR COURT.

Realizing that I am separated from God and that He has made a way for me to know Him personally, what must I do? There are four steps I would like to point out.

1. REALIZE THAT YOU ARE A SINNER.

You must admit your spiritual need. Stop making excuses, blaming everyone and everything else for your actions, and accept responsibility.

10

2. RECOGNIZE THAT JESUS CHRIST DIED ON THAT CROSS FOR YOU.

The Bible tells us, "For Christ died for sins once for all, the righteous for the unrighteous, to bring you to God" (1 Pet. 3:18 NIV). He paid the price for your sin. The apostle Paul acknowledged, "The life which I now live in the flesh I live by faith in the Son of God, who loved me and gave Himself for me" (Gal. 2:20).

3. REPENT OF YOUR SIN.

The word "repent" means "to change your direction." The Bible tells us, "Repent therefore and be converted, that your sins may be blotted out, so that times of refreshing may come from the presence of the Lord" (Acts 3:19). God commands people everywhere to repent. You must be willing to have changes take place in your life and be willing to turn away from those things that displease God.

4. COME TO AND RECEIVE JESUS CHRIST.

Jesus said, "Come here to me, all who are growing weary to the point of exhaustion, and who have been loaded with burdens and are bending beneath their weight, and I alone will cause you to cease from your labor and take away your burdens and thus refresh you with rest" (Matt. 11:28 WUEST'S).

It is essential that you come to Jesus as you are. Don't try to "clean up your life" before you come to God. Instead, come to Him as you are and He'll do the "cleaning." Jesus said, "The one who comes to Me I will by no means cast out" (John 6:37).

Becoming a Christian is more than merely believing a creed or trying to live by certain standards. Becoming a Christian is personally receiving Jesus Christ into one's heart and life as both Savior and Lord. Jesus said "Behold, I stand at the door and knock. If anyone hears My voice and opens the door, I will come in to him and dine with him, and he with Me" (Rev. 3:20).

The Bible also tells us, "As many as received Him, to them He gave the right to become children of God" (John 1:12). Are you ready to do that?

A SUGGESTED PRAYER

Would you like to receive Jesus Christ into your heart and life right now? If so, you might pray a prayer like this:

LORD JESUS, I KNOW THAT I AM A SINNER, AND I AM SORRY FOR MY SIN. I THANK YOU FOR DYING ON THAT CROSS FOR ME. I TURN FROM MY SIN AND I TURN TO YOU BY FAITH RIGHT NOW. FORGIVE ME FOR ALL OF IT. FILL ME WITH THE POWER OF YOUR HOLY SPIRIT. I WANT TO BE YOUR DISCIPLE. HELP ME TO LOVE YOU AND HATE SIN FROM THIS TIME FORWARD. THANK YOU FOR YOUR OFFER OF FORGIVENESS. I GLADLY ACCEPT IT NOW. IN JESUS' NAME I PRAY, AMEN.

If you just prayed that prayer and really meant it, Jesus Christ has now taken residence in your heart! Not only that, but He has forgiven you of all your sin. The Bible tells us, "If we confess our sins, He is faithful and just to forgive us our sins and to cleanse us from all unrighteousness" (1 John 1:9). God also promises, "As far as the east is from the west, so far has He removed our transgressions from us" (Ps. 103:12).

God has taken your sin and has cast it into the "sea of forgetfulness," posting a sign that says, "No fishing allowed!" Think of it! Your past is behind you, and God now has an incredible plan just for you. He tells us, "For I know the thoughts that I think toward you, says the LORD, thoughts of peace and not of evil, to give you a future and a hope" (Jer. 29:11).

Together let's discover how to walk with God in this plan He has for us.

When the Creator of the universe takes residence in your heart, you are going to know it.

"Just the Facts, Ma'am!"

Now that you have made this commitment, or recommitment, to Jesus Christ, it is important that you understand what God has done. Since you have come to Him on His terms, He has forgiven you of your sin. As a part of that process, He has also *justified* you. Scripture tells us that we are "being justified freely by His grace through the redemption that is in Christ Jesus" (Rom. 3:24).

What does that mean? Well, the word "justified" means, "Something has been made right." You have been put in a right relationship with the God from whom you had been separated. One explanation of justification is, "It's just as if it had never happened." This means that not only has your sin been forgiven and your guilt removed, but that you are going to Heaven!

13

Remember that Jesus said, "Everyone who believes in Him—who cleaves to Him, trusts Him, and relies on Him—may not *perish, but* have eternal life *and* [actually] live forever" (John 3:15 AMP).

You do need to know something else. Just as surely as there is a God who desperately loves you, there is also a devil who intensely hates you. You may have thought that the devil was merely some fictitious figure. But according to the Bible, he is a real and very powerful spirit being who is opposed to what God is doing. Though he is far from being God's equal, he is powerful nonetheless, and he would like to rob you of what has taken place in your life now that you have accepted Jesus Christ.

Jesus showed us just how this works in a story he told, "The Parable of the Sower."

> Then he told them many things in parables, saying: "A farmer went out to sow his seed. As he was scattering the seed, some fell along the path, and the birds came and ate it up. Some fell on rocky places, where it did not have much soil. It sprang up quickly, because the soil was shallow. But when the sun came up, the plants were scorched, and they withered because they had no root. Other seed fell among thorns, which grew up and choked the plants. Still other seed fell on good soil, where it produced a crop—a hundred, sixty or thirty times what was sown."
>
> Matt. 13:3–8 NIV

Jesus told this parable to show four different reactions to the message of the gospel. He then proceeded to give the meaning behind it.

14

> "Listen then to what the parable of the sower means: When anyone hears the message about the kingdom and does not understand it, the evil one comes and snatches away what was sown in his heart. This is the seed sown along the path. What was sown on rocky places is the man who hears the word and at once receives it with joy. But since he has no root, he lasts only a short time. When trouble or persecution comes because of the word, he quickly falls away. What was sown among the thorns is the man who hears the word, but the worries of this life and the deceitfulness of wealth choke it, making it unfruitful. What was sown on good soil is the man who hears the word and understands it. He produces a crop, yielding a hundred, sixty or thirty times what was sown."
>
> Matt. 13:18–23 NIV

We can learn many valuable lessons about spiritual growth in this parable. In the first comparison we see how the devil immediately tries to stop any spiritual growth in a person's life. Jesus' second comparison is interesting. Here

he describes the person who has apparently had a great emotional experience with God, but as soon as the going gets a bit rough, he throws in the towel. Is that going to happen to you?

It doesn't have to if you don't want it to. For some people, accepting Jesus Christ is a very emotional experience. They may feel ecstatic joy about this new relationship or deep sorrow for the sins they had committed, but we know that the Lord has come into our lives not because of what we *feel* but rather because of what we *know!* The Bible reassures us, "These things I have written to you who believe in the name of the Son of God, that you may *know* that you have eternal life" (1 John 5:13).

Notice that the verse does not say, "You may hope that you have eternal life if God's in a really good mood that particular day," or "You may know that you have eternal life if you had a really great emotional experience." This wonderful promise of eternal life is based upon God's promise to you. You have His word on it. And there is only one thing that God cannot do: lie.

Jesus next identifies the person who appears to believe in Jesus Christ, but other things soon choke out this belief. First appearances can be deceiving. To repeat, some will reject the gospel message outright because they want nothing to do with God; with their cooperation, Satan will not allow the gospel to have any impact on them at all. Others will seem to accept the message gladly, but soon fall away because they had only a superficial religious experience and were never really born again. Still others seem to accept the gospel yet hold on to the old life and its ways; their faith will eventually dissipate. The truth is they never really had any faith to begin with.

But others will truly believe. Initially they may not appear to be the greatest prospects. They may not have the

most immediately "profound" conversion. Their initial growth may not be as dramatic, but time will reveal that they are the true believers. It is my sincere hope that you will be the person represented in the last category—that you will be "seed sown on good ground."

**We do not know God has come into our lives
because of what we *feel*,
but because of what we *know*.**

Steps to Spiritual Growth

❖ ❖ ❖ ❖ ❖ ❖ ❖

THERE ARE FOUR STEPS YOU CAN TAKE TO HELP YOU BE THAT GOOD GROUND.

ꙮ PRAY

Now that you have come into a personal relationship with the God who loves you and has a unique plan for your life, you need to become better acquainted with Him! One way to do this is through prayer. Prayer is both talking and listening to God. It is one of the ultimate tests of a person's relationship with and commitment to Jesus Christ. After Paul's conversion, it was said of him, "Behold, he is praying" (Acts 9:11).

You might wonder if there is a certain posture for prayer, but in the Bible people prayed standing, lifting their hands, sitting, lying down, kneeling, lifting their eyes, and bowing—any posture will do. The main thing is to pray!

You might also wonder if there is a certain place you should pray—in a church, for instance. Though that is a good place to pray, in the Bible we read that people prayed during battle, in a cave, in a closet, in a garden, on a mountainside, by a river, by the sea, in the street, in bed, in a home, in a prison, in the wilderness, and even in a fish! The apostle Paul declares, "I desire that the men pray everywhere" (1 Tim. 2:8).

You might even wonder when it is the best time to pray. In the Bible people are found praying early in the morning, in mid-morning, in the evening, three times a day, before meals, after meals, at bedtime, at midnight, day and night. We also learn of people praying when they're young, when they're old, when they're in trouble, every day, and always.

Prayer is good in any posture, at any time, in any place, under all circumstances. Prayer is needed in the life of the person who wants to know Jesus Christ in a personal way. The Bible tells us, "Pray without ceasing, in everything give thanks; for this is the will of God in Christ Jesus for you" (1 Thess. 5:17–18).

Jesus told us that "men always ought to pray and not lose heart" (Luke 18:1). When you face difficulties in life and find yourself worried about the future, that's the time to pray! We are also told, "Be anxious for nothing, but in everything by prayer and supplication, with thanksgiving, let your requests be made known to God; and the peace of God, which surpasses all understanding, will guard your hearts and minds through Christ Jesus" (Phil. 4:6).

There are basically four different types of prayer:

18

Petition—when we bring our own prayer needs to God. "[Cast] all your care upon Him, for He cares for you" (1 Pet. 5:7).

Supplication and Intercession—where we pray for the needs of others. "Therefore confess your sins to each other and pray for each other that you may be healed. The prayer of a righteous man is powerful and effective" (James 5:16 NIV).

Praise, Thanksgiving, and Worship—when we take time to thank God for what He has done in our lives and get to know Him better by learning to worship Him in the process. "I will bless the Lord at all times; His praise shall continually be in my mouth" (Ps. 34:1). "Oh, give thanks to the LORD, for He is good! For His mercy endures forever" (Ps. 106:1).

Confession—where I admit my own sins and shortcomings to God. "If we confess our sins, He is faithful and just to forgive us our sins and to cleanse us from all unrighteousness"

(1 John. 1:9). This type of prayer is extremely important because unconfessed sin can hinder your prayers. "If I regard iniquity in my heart, the Lord will not hear [me]" (Ps. 66:18).

To confess means "to agree with God." It means, in essence, to see things the way He sees them. For instance, I know that God hates sin, so if I am "confessing" my sin, I should want to turn away from it. Scripture tells us, "You who love the LORD, hate evil" (Ps. 97:10).

One of the keys to learning how to pray is to know God better. One way to get to know God better is to read the Bible. Just remember that you can pray to God about anything, anytime, anywhere.

Anything

For blessings .... 1 Chron. 4:10

For help in trouble .... 2 Chron. 14:11

To express love to God .... Ps. 18:1

When in anguish .... Ps. 22:1–2

To express thanks to God .... Ps. 52:9

For direction .... Ps. 143:8

For instruction .... Ps. 143:10

In praise and worship .... Ps. 145:1–2

For guidance .... Prov. 3:5–6

For daily needs .... Matt. 6:11

For God's mercy .... Luke 18:13

For your ministry .... John 15:16

For someone's salvation .... Rom. 10:1

For EVERYTHING .... Phil. 4:6–7

For wisdom .... James 1:5

For physical healing .... James 5:16

For forgiveness .... 1 John 1:9

For ANYTHING .... 1 John 5:14

19

Anytime

When you're "up" ....Ex. 15:11–13

When you're "down" ....2 Sam. 12:15

In spiritual battle ....1 Kings 18:36

When you've sinned ....Ps. 51:3–4

Evening, morning, and noon ....Ps. 55:17

When in trials ....Acts 16:25

Anywhere

In the house of God ....1 Sam. 1:9–10

In your room ....Matt. 6:6

Out in the hills ....Matt. 14:23

With others ....Matt. 18:19–20

Alone ....Mark 1:35

Prayer is not getting my will in heaven, but God's will on earth.

20 READ THE BIBLE

Have you ever purchased a product that comes with a set of instructions? If you're like me, you disregard them and put the thing together without ever even looking at the instructions—and, like me, you spend a great deal of time taking apart those things you've put together hastily without consulting the manual.

Did you know that God has given us a manual for life? In fact, everything you need to know about God and how to live life to its fullest is found in its pages. It's called the Bible.

A poll printed in *USA Today* revealed that 93 percent of 662 people interviewed said they owned at least one Bible. Of that percentage, however, only 55 percent said they read their Bible, and only 25 percent said they did so every day. Yet, in reality, success or failure in the Christian life depends on how much of the Bible we get into our hearts and minds on a daily basis and on how obedient we are to it. If we neglect the study

of the Scripture, our spiritual life will ultimately unravel. Everything we need to know about God is taught in the Bible.

Abraham Lincoln said, "All the good from the Savior of the world is communicated through this book. All things that are desirable to man are contained in it." Honest Abe was exactly right!

The Bible is not just one book; it's actually sixty-six books written by more than forty different authors over a period of 1,500 years. These authors include a wide spectrum of people, from "blue collar workers" to the most powerful world leaders ever to walk the face of the earth. They include kings, statesmen, prophets, rabbis, a physician, a tax collector, a farmer, and a fisherman. Still—and this is important to note—the real author of the Bible is God Himself. In 2 Timothy 3:16 we are told that all Scripture is "God-breathed," meaning that even though humans wrote it out on paper, the ultimate source was God. God worked through the authors of the Bible much like an artist uses different types of brushes when he paints. Each has its place in the finished painting.

21

TIPS FOR BIBLE STUDY

Tip #1 Don't Read Haphazardly

It is important that you read a book of the Bible from beginning to end. Some people "flip around" through the pages of Scripture with no real rhyme or reason. They may start it off with a helping of Matthew, throw in a little Daniel, sprinkle it with some Exodus, and finish off with a dash of Revelation. But the end result will be spiritual indigestion!

I suggest you begin your Bible study with the Gospel of John. It is the gripping and powerful story of the life, ministry, and teachings of Jesus Christ. (It is included in this book.) After that, you may just read through the remainder of the New Testament, then come back and pick up the other three Gospels (Matthew, Mark, and Luke).

Tip #2 Pray

Remember, God is the author of Scripture, so it's a good idea to pray before you read His Word. The Bible encourages us to do that. We are told that we should "call out for insight" and "cry out for understanding," studying God's Word as though we were mining for some "hidden treasure" (Prov. 2:3–4).

Psalm 119:18 says, "Open my eyes, that I may see wondrous things from Your law." Before we open the Bible, we need to come before the Lord and say something like, "Father, I believe You are the author of this Book. I believe, as You say in scripture, that all scripture is inspired by You. Therefore, I am asking You, as the author of the Book, to take me on a guided tour. Help me to understand, and show me how these truths apply in my life." That form of sincere prayer will cause the Bible to come alive in your time of study.

Tip #3 Remember

22

Another important way to get the most out of Bible study is to commit what you find in it to memory. Once scripture is ingrained in your memory, it will always be there. You'll find that there are times when the verses you memorized will pay great dividends. They will bring comfort to your heart and strength in times of intense temptation. We're told in Psalm 119:11, "Your Word I have hidden in my heart, that I might not sin against You."

Although it is good to carry a Bible in your briefcase, pocket, or purse, the best place to carry it is in your heart. In Deuteronomy 11:18–20, God instructs us to "lay up" or fix His words in our hearts and minds, to teach them to our children, and to write them down.

For me, the best way to remember things is to write them down. When I write something down, it is more deeply engraved into my memory than if I just read it. I may not even have to refer back to

what I wrote. Writing something down seems to give it more "staying power" in my mind. It is a good practice to keep a journal or notebook with your Bible. When you study the Scripture and a passage personally speaks to you, write down what God has shown you. Maybe it won't be useful right at that moment, but the next day, or the next month, it might be just what you need.

Tip #4 Chew Your Food Carefully

When reading, it is also very important to meditate, or stop and think about, what the Lord may be showing you. It's good to chew your spiritual food. That is what is meant by meditating on the Word. We are better off reading five verses slowly and understanding what they mean than reading five chapters quickly and not getting anything out of it. Learn to slow down. Learn to meditate on what you've read. Learn to allow the Holy Spirit to speak to you through a given passage. The man who is given to us as an example of walking with God in Psalm 1 meditates in His word day and night. That's excellent advice.

23

Tip #5 Find Where the Rubber Meets the Road

Finally, we come to the importance of application. Jesus said, "If you abide in My word, you are My disciples indeed" (John 8:31). It's not enough to study the Scripture on a daily basis, or even to memorize it. It must affect the way that we live. It's not enough to go through the Word of God; the Word of God must go through you! It's not how you mark your Bible, it's how your Bible marks you!

The word "abide" Jesus used in the above verse is the same word He uses in John 15:7, where He says, "If you abide in Me, and My words abide in you, you will ask what you desire, and it shall be done for you." The word "abide" means "to stay in a given place, to draw strength and resources from the Lord." Jesus used the analogy of a vine drawing its resources from the soil and the branch drawing its resources from the vine.

In the same way, we are to maintain unbroken fellowship, communion, and friendship with God. If we are abiding in the Word, it means that we're drawing our ideas and lifestyle from the Word, and our actions and speech are also being affected.

Colossians 3:16 says, "Let the word of Christ dwell in you richly." This means to let the word of Christ be perfectly at home in you. God wants His Word to permeate every area of your life—your home, your business, your play time, and your prayer time. Continuing in the Word is a necessity for all who wish to know and follow Jesus Christ as His disciple.

There are many benefits to be received from reading and studying God's Word. A few are listed below.

Makes us prosper; gives us success ....Josh. 1:8
Restores the soul; makes wise the simple
....Ps. 19:7
Rejoices the heart ....Ps. 19:8
Provides warnings; provides rewards ......Ps. 19:11
Keeps us from slipping ....Ps. 37:31
Keeps our ways pure; keeps us from sin
....Ps. 119:9, 11
Provides delight; provides counsel ....Ps. 119:24
Gives comfort in affliction ....Ps. 119:50
Makes us wise ....Ps. 119:98; 2 Tim. 3:15
Guides us ....Prov. 6:22
Provides spiritual nourishment ....Matt. 4:4
Sanctifies us ....John 15:3; 17:17
Helps our faith ....John 20:30-31
Gives us hope for the future ....Rom. 15:4
Teaches, rebukes, corrects, trains, equips
....2 Tim. 3:16–17
Makes us grow to spiritual maturity ......1 Pet. 2:2

24

It is not how you mark your Bible that matters, but how your Bible marks you.

¢ GET TOGETHER IN FELLOWSHIP WITH BELIEVERS

The third building block is friendships with other committed Christians. One could liken it to a group of coals burning brightly together. Each one not only emanates its own heat, but helps to keep the others hot and benefits from their warmth as well. Being with other Christians affects our lives in a similar way. You build up other believers while they build you up!

Coming back to the burning coal analogy, if you were to isolate one piece of coal from the others, it would only be a matter of time until that coal's heat would dissipate. You as a Christian are the same. You need other Christians in your life to help keep your spiritual fire burning, and they need you in theirs. The Bible tells us, "And let us consider how we may spur one another on toward love and good deeds. Let us not give up meeting together, as some are in the habit of doing, but let us encourage one another—and all the more as you see the Day approaching" (Heb. 10:24– 25 NIV).

25

The Book of Acts is the story of the beginning of the church. Acts 2:42 gives a brief description of what took place in the early church, giving us the secret to a thriving, growing church: "They continued steadily learning the teaching of the apostles, and joined in their fellowship, in the breaking of bread, and in prayer" (PHILLIPS). From this verse we see three important reasons to be involved in a strong, Bible-teaching church. We also see the benefit such a church can bring to our spiritual lives.

CHURCH IS A PLACE TO LEARN.

The early believers placed a strong emphasis on learning what the Bible says. If we want to grow spiritually, we must do the same. The Bible tells us that God has given us pastors, teachers, and evangelists (among other Christian

leaders in the church) to help us mature in our Christian walk (see Eph. 4:11). For that reason, we should take full advantage of the people God has placed in leadership, making the most of every opportunity to study under their teaching.

WE NEED TO GO TO CHURCH ON A REGULAR BASIS.

Again, these early Christians "continued steadily," or steadfastly, in their worship. This was not a casual attitude, as one might have joining a social club. These believers had a spiritual excitement in what they were doing, and they applied themselves to what was being taught from the Word. Healthy Christians will be hungry Christians—hungry for God's Word. The Bible, speaking about our desire for His Word, says, "As newborn babes, desire the pure milk of the word, that you may grow" (1 Pet. 2:2).

CHURCH IS A PLACE TO PRAY WITH OTHERS AND WORSHIP THE LORD.

For a dramatic illustration about what God will do when His people pray together, look at the story of Acts 12. The Bible tells us that God inhabits the praises of His people (see Ps. 22:3). And Jesus says, "For where two or three are gathered together in My name, I am there in the midst of them" (Matt. 18:20). God clearly works in a special way when His people are gathered together.

Fellowship is not just Christian social activity.

CHURCH IS A PLACE TO DEVELOP AND USE THE GIFTS THAT GOD HAS GIVEN TO YOU.

Romans 12 tells us that "Just as each of us has one body with many members, and these members do not all have the same function, so in Christ we who are many form one body...We have different gifts, according to the grace given us" (Rom. 12:4, 6 NIV). Going to church should not be a pas-

sive experience, but a time when we can learn what spiritual gifts God has given us—serving, teaching, encouraging, giving—and then use those gifts for the glory of God.

TELL OTHERS

As a result of what the Holy Spirit is doing in your life as you get to know God better by reading His Word, spending time with Him in prayer, and growing together with other believers, you will want to let others know what He has done for you. Jesus told us to go into the world and preach the gospel to every person.

The apostle Paul was so compelled to tell others about Jesus Christ. He gives us a good example to follow in his letter to the Colossians:

"Naturally, we proclaim Christ! We warn everyone we meet, and we teach everyone we can, all that we know about him, so that...we may bring every man up to his full maturity in Christ" (Col. 1:28 PHILLIPS).

The best way to prepare yourself for telling others about your newfound faith is to saturate yourself with the Bible. And when you share the gospel, you will find that God uses His Word in a powerful way. God says of His own word, "My word...shall not return to Me void, but it shall accomplish what I please" (Isa. 55:11). There is a special authority in the words of Scripture.

Good News!

If someone asks you a question you don't know how to answer, don't be embarrassed to admit it. Tell that person that you'll get an answer, and then ask your pastor or a Christian friend who has known the Lord longer than you. The Bible tells us, "Always be prepared to give an answer to everyone who asks you to give the reason for the hope that you have" (1 Pet. 3:15 NIV).

27

This will not happen overnight, but don't be discouraged! Every day as you grow closer to Jesus and learn more of His Word, you will become spiritually stronger, and you will be better able to share your newfound faith.

One powerful tool in your "evangelistic toolbox" is your own story of how you came to know Jesus. This is often referred to as one's "testimony." No one knows your own story as well as you do. Tell others how you used to think before Jesus came into your life, and then tell them the changes that have taken place since. I'd encourage you to read the Book of Acts and notice how the apostle Paul used his personal story time after time to build a rapport with those to whom he was speaking.

Paul told us, "I am not ashamed of the gospel of Christ, for it is the power of God to salvation for everyone who believes" (Rom. 1:16). Take time to commit the basic gospel message to memory. Then ask the Lord to open opportunities for you to share your new faith with someone today. The Bible says that we need to "be ready in season and out of season" to tell others about God and His Word (see 2 Tim. 4:2). You never know when those moments of opportunity will come!

28

One of the greatest arguments for Christianity is a transformed life.

Trials

As a result of growing spiritually as a Christian, you will experience what the Bible calls "trials." Speaking of this, the Bible says, "In this you greatly rejoice, though now for a little while, if need be, you have been grieved by various trials, that the genuineness of your faith, being more precious than gold that perishes, though it is tested by fire, may be found to praise, honor, and glory at the revelation of Jesus Christ" (1 Pet. 1:6–7).

During these times in your Christian life, you may not feel the presence of God. But remember that your relationship with God is not based on how you feel, but on what He's done and said. It is during times when we do not feel the presence of God that we learn to walk with Jesus Christ by faith instead of feelings.

Trials are a bit like clouds that obscure the rays of the sun. When you see clouds, it doesn't mean the sun is not shining; it simply means that you cannot feel the sun's rays at that particular time. Clouds and spiritual storms may come and go, but hang in there and realize that it's all a part of growing spiritually.

God wants spiritual fruit to come from your life, meaning He wants to develop character in you as you become more like Jesus. This "fruit" or the practical results of a changed life will be clearly visible to others, and fruit doesn't usually grow on mountain tops, but in the valleys. If most of us could have our way, we would live perpetually on spiritual mountain tops, feeling God's presence and having everything go our way. But it is during the tough times of trials that we deepen and grow. James, in his epistle, tells us,

When all kinds of trials and temptations crowd into your lives, my brothers, don't resent them as intruders, but welcome them as friends! Realize that they come to test your faith and to produce in you the quality of endurance. But let the process go on until that endurance is fully developed, and you will find you have become men of mature character.

James 1:2–3 PHILLIPS

To see what sort of trials the great men and women of the Bible had to go through, read Hebrews 11. You will also learn a great deal about how God uses trials and setbacks in our lives by reading the exciting story of Joseph in Genesis 37, 39–45.

Temptation

Now that you are following Jesus Christ, you will find that Satan will try to trip you up with temptation. Yet testing and temptation can have a positive effect! If we really want to follow God, it will make us cling to Him all the tighter. If not, we'll let go and fall.

Remember the Parable of the Sower we discussed earlier? The seed sown on rocky ground withered because it had no roots. In much the same way, people who say they have accepted Jesus Christ into their lives, perhaps even through a great emotional experience, display their true shallowness by "throwing in the towel" during times of testing, temptation, and persecution.

It is important for you to know that as a Christian you have come under the protection of God. Jesus told us that we are His sheep, and no one will be able to "snatch [us] out of [His] hand" (John 10:28). Of course, the devil doesn't want you to know this. He would like you to think he can "pick you off" at will. But it simply is not true!

One of the greatest promises concerning temptation to be found in the Bible is 1 Corinthians 10:13:

> No temptation has overtaken you except such as is common to man; but God is faithful, who will not allow you to be tempted beyond what you are able, but with the temptation will also make the way of escape, that you may be able to bear it.

In other words, God will not allow you to go through more than you can handle! He knows what your breaking point is, so the temptation that He allows in your life will be graded to the fiber of your spiritual character.

Sometimes people will not accept responsibility for giving in to temptation's pull. "The devil made me do it!" they exclaim. Of course, this is nothing new. It dates clear back to the Garden of Eden, when Adam disobeyed God and ate of the forbidden fruit. After Adam was asked by the Lord if he had done this, he replied, "The woman...gave me of the tree" (Gen. 3:12). Meanwhile, Eve, not wanting to bear the blame, squarely blamed her disobedience on the devil who had tempted her.

Though others may tempt us (and certainly the devil plays a key part in it), we must recognize that he needs our cooperation if he is to be successful.

The tempter (Satan) needs cooperation from the "temptee" (you). Scripture has explained, "A man is tempted when he is drawn away by his own desires and is enticed."

So what is the best remedy against temptation? The Bible tells us to flee from the temptations of this life and to pursue righteousness (see 1 Tim. 6:11). The best way to keep from going backward is to go forward! Or, as the Bible has assured, "Walk in the Spirit, and you shall not fulfill the lust of the flesh" (Gal. 5:16). The best defense is a good offense.

If you want to be strong when faced with temptation, continue to concentrate on what you have just read. Spend time in the study and memorization of Scripture and in prayer. Make time to be with God's people regularly in a strong church, and develop and use the talents and gifts God has given you. Finally, look for opportunities to share what Jesus Christ has done for you with others.

It is not a sin to be tempted—it's only a sin when you give in to temptation.

The Secret to Spiritual Growth

❖   ❖   ❖   ❖   ❖   ❖

There are two important secrets to spiritual growth
—the Holy Spirit and patience.

THE HOLY SPIRIT

Right now you might feel overwhelmed with
all you've just learned. You may even be thinking,
"How can I keep from failing as a Christian if I
always made a mess of things in the past?" I
have some good news for you. You see, there is
a dimension of power that is available for every
believer—a power that will guide you, give you
boldness in your witness, and empower you to
be the Christian God wants you to be. When we become
Christians, the Holy Spirit takes up residence inside us,
giving us the assurance that we are children of God.

No, this isn't some "ghost" or a strange sensation that
comes over you. The Holy Spirit has been described as the
"Comforter," the "Counselor," the "Spirit of Truth," the "Spirit
of God," the "Spirit of Life," and the "Spirit of Wisdom" (John
14:26, 15:26, 16:13; Gen. 1:2; Rom. 8:2; Isa. 11:2). Jesus
emphasized the need for the Holy Spirit's power in our lives
when He told His disciples, "But you will receive power
when the Holy Spirit comes on you; and you will be my witnesses in Jerusalem, and in all Judea and Samaria, and to the
ends of the earth" (Acts 1:8 NIV).

Now that's some mandate! And this was an unusual
group of ordinary (and sometimes wishy-washy) men. But
Jesus knew they could become His witnesses to the ends of

33

the earth with the help of the Holy Spirit. And they did! In fact, those same disciples who fled after Jesus' arrest before His crucifixion were able to face even the most difficult of circumstances without flinching in their faith. Some even died for their beliefs.

It's not hard to be a Christian—it's *impossible,* without the power of the Holy Spirit. The only effective way to live the Christian life and be a witness for Jesus Christ is through and by the power of the Holy Spirit. The Bible admonishes us to "be filled with the Spirit" (Eph. 5:18). The Greek word used for "be filled" implies a continual filling, so ask Jesus to daily fill you with His Holy Spirit. You will notice a tremendous difference in the way you are able to face life's problems and live your Christian witness.

It's not hard to be a Christian—it's *impossible,* without the power of the Holy Spirit.

---

34 ◆ BE PATIENT

If you're at all like me, you're always looking for a shortcut or the path of least resistance in getting something done. In our technologically advanced times where we can get things accomplished at the press of a button, it is easy to carry this "give it to me now" mentality into our spiritual life. We think, "How do I put this thing on the fast track? What's the easiest and fastest way to grow spiritually?"

The answer is, there are no shortcuts to spiritual growth and maturity. It takes time and commitment. But it is certainly time well spent! You wouldn't go to a gym or a health club one time and expect to come out immediately with a fully developed physique, would you? In the same way, as you consistently apply the principles I've shared with you in your relationship with Jesus, you will see gradual, but real change in your life.

Jesus promises, "He who abides in Me, and I in him, bears much fruit" (John 15:5). The word "abide" means "a

permanence of position; maintaining unbroken fellowship with another." And what is the fruit Jesus is talking about? Among other things, it includes changes in your life, character, and conduct over the passing of time.

You may not see the distinct changes taking place in your life as quickly as others do. If you were to pull up a chair in front of a peach tree to watch the growth of the fruit, you wouldn't be able to see any dramatic changes before your eyes. But if you were to look at it every few days, you would eventually see some definite changes. The same will happen to you spiritually as you get to know Jesus Christ. So bloom where you are planted! In time you will discover the joy of a bountiful harvest.

The Christian life is not a sprint, but a long distance run.

35

How Do You Know If You Are a Christian?

1. Do you confess Jesus as Lord? 1 John 4:15

2. Are you unhappy or miserable when you are sinning? 1 John 3:9

3. Do you enjoy fellowship with other believers? 1 John 5:1

4. Do you obey Christ's commands? 1 John 5:3

5. Do you love God's Word? 1 John 2:5

If you answered yes to the questions above, then you can know that you are a Christian.

THE GOSPEL OF JOHN

NEW KING JAMES VERSION

John 1

❖ ❖ ❖ ❖ ❖ ❖ ❖

1   In the beginning was the Word, and the Word was with God, and the Word was God.

2   He was in the beginning with God.

3   All things were made through Him, and without Him nothing was made that was made.

4   In Him was life, and the life was the light of men.

5   And the light shines in the darkness, and the darkness did not comprehend it.

6   There was a man sent from God, whose name was John.

7   This man came for a witness, to bear witness of the Light, that all through him might believe.

8   He was not that Light, but was sent to bear witness of that Light.

9   That was the true Light which gives light to every man who comes into the world.

10 He was in the world, and the world was made through Him, and the world did not know Him.

11 He came to His own, and His own did not receive Him.

12 But as many as received Him, to them He gave the right to become children of God, even to those who believe in His name:

13 who were born, not of blood, nor of the will of the flesh, nor of the will of man, but of God.

14 And the Word became flesh and dwelt among us, and we beheld His glory, the glory as of the only begotten of the Father, full of grace and truth.

15 John bore witness of Him and cried out, saying, "This was He of whom I said, 'He who comes after me is preferred before me, for He was before me.'"

16 And of His fullness we have all received, and grace for grace.

17 For the law was given through Moses, but grace and truth came through Jesus Christ.

18 No one has seen God at any time. The only begotten Son, who is in the bosom of the Father, He has declared Him.

19 Now this is the testimony of John, when the Jews sent priests and Levites from Jerusalem to ask him, "Who are you?"

20 He confessed, and did not deny, but confessed, "I am not the Christ."

21 And they asked him, "What then? Are you Elijah?" He said, "I am not." "Are you the Prophet?" And he answered, "No."

22 Then they said to him, "Who are you, that we may give an answer to those who sent us? What do you say about yourself?"

23 He said: "I am 'The voice of one crying in the wilderness: "Make straight the way of the Lord,"' as the prophet Isaiah said."

24 Now those who were sent were from the Pharisees.

25 And they asked him, saying, "Why then do you baptize if you are not the Christ, nor Elijah, nor the Prophet?"

39

26 John answered them, saying, "I baptize with water, but there stands One among you whom you do not know.

27 "It is He who, coming after me, is preferred before me, whose sandal strap I am not worthy to loose."

28 These things were done in Bethabara beyond the Jordan, where John was baptizing.

29 The next day John saw Jesus coming toward him, and said, "Behold! The Lamb of God who takes away the sin of the world!

30 "This is He of whom I said, 'After me comes a Man who is preferred before me, for He was before me.'

31 "I did not know Him; but that He should be revealed to Israel, therefore I came baptizing with water."

32 And John bore witness, saying, "I saw the Spirit descending from heaven like a dove, and He remained upon Him.

33 "I did not know Him, but He who sent me to baptize with water said to me, 'Upon whom you see the Spirit

descending, and remaining on Him, this is He who baptizes with the Holy Spirit.'

34 "And I have seen and testified that this is the Son of God."

35 Again, the next day, John stood with two of his disciples.

36 And looking at Jesus as He walked, he said, "Behold the Lamb of God!"

37 The two disciples heard him speak, and they followed Jesus.

38 Then Jesus turned, and seeing them following, said to them, "What do you seek?" They said to Him, "Rabbi" (which is to say, when translated, Teacher), "where are You staying?"

39 He said to them, "Come and see." They came and saw where He was staying, and remained with Him that day (now it was about the tenth hour).

40 One of the two who heard John speak, and followed Him, was Andrew, Simon Peter's brother.

41 He first found his own brother Simon, and said to him, "We have found the Messiah" (which is translated, the Christ).

42 And he brought him to Jesus. Now when Jesus looked at him, He said, "You are Simon the son of Jonah. You shall be called Cephas" (which is translated, A Stone).

43 The following day Jesus wanted to go to Galilee, and He found Philip and said to him, "Follow Me."

44 Now Philip was from Bethsaida, the city of Andrew and Peter.

45 Philip found Nathanael and said to him, "We have found Him of whom Moses in the law, and also the prophets, wrote—Jesus of Nazareth, the son of Joseph."

46 And Nathanael said to him, "Can anything good come out of Nazareth?" Philip said to him, "Come and see."

47 Jesus saw Nathanael coming toward Him, and said of him, "Behold, an Israelite indeed, in whom is no guile!"

48 Nathanael said to Him, "How do You know me?" Jesus answered and said to him, "Before Philip called you, when you were under the fig tree, I saw you."

49 Nathanael answered and said to Him, "Rabbi, You are the Son of God! You are the King of Israel!"

50 Jesus answered and said to him, "Because I said to you, 'I saw you under the fig tree,' do you believe? You will see greater things than these."

51 And He said to him, "Most assuredly, I say to you, hereafter you shall see heaven open, and the angels of God ascending and descending upon the Son of Man."

John 2

1 On the third day there was a wedding in Cana of Galilee, and the mother of Jesus was there.

2 Now both Jesus and His disciples were invited to the wedding.

3 And when they ran out of wine, the mother of Jesus said to Him, "They have no wine."

4 Jesus said to her, "Woman, what does your concern have to do with Me? My hour has not yet come."

5 His mother said to the servants, "Whatever He says to you, do it."

6 Now there were set there six waterpots of stone, according to the manner of purification of the Jews, containing twenty or thirty gallons apiece.

7 Jesus said to them, "Fill the waterpots with water." And they filled them up to the brim.

8 And He said to them, "Draw some out now, and take it to the master of the feast." And they took it.

9 When the master of the feast had tasted the water that was made wine, and did not know where it came from (but the servants who had drawn the water knew), the master of the feast called the bridegroom.

10 And he said to him, "Every man at the beginning sets out the good wine, and when the guests have well drunk, then that which is inferior; but you have kept the good wine until now."

11 This beginning of signs Jesus did in Cana of Galilee, and manifested His glory; and His disciples believed in Him.

12 After this He went down to Capernaum, He, His mother, His brothers, and His disciples; and they did not stay there many days.

13 Now the Passover of the Jews was at hand, and Jesus went up to Jerusalem.

14 And He found in the temple those who sold oxen and sheep and doves, and the moneychangers doing business.

15 When He had made a whip of cords, He drove them all out of the temple, with the sheep and the oxen, and poured out the changers' money and overturned the tables.

16 And He said to those who sold doves, "Take these things away! Do not make My Father's house a house of merchandise!"

17 Then His disciples remembered that it was written, "Zeal for Your house has eaten Me up."

18 So the Jews answered and said to Him, "What sign do You show to us, since You do these things?"

19 Jesus answered and said to them, "Destroy this temple, and in three days I will raise it up."

20 Then the Jews said, "It has taken forty-six years to build this temple, and will You raise it up in three days?"

21 But He was speaking of the temple of His body.

22 Therefore, when He had risen from the dead, His disciples remembered that He had said this to them; and they believed the Scripture and the word which Jesus had said.

23 Now when He was in Jerusalem at the Passover, during the feast, many believed in His name when they saw the signs which He did.

24 But Jesus did not commit Himself to them, because He knew all men,

25 and had no need that anyone should testify of man, for He knew what was in man.

John 3

◆   ◆   ◆   ◆   ◆   ◆   ◆

1   There was a man of the Pharisees named Nicodemus, a
    ruler of the Jews.
2   This man came to Jesus by night and said to Him,
    "Rabbi, we know that You are a teacher come from God;
    for no one can do these signs that You do unless God is
    with him."
3   Jesus answered and said to him, "Most assuredly, I say
    to you, unless one is born again, he cannot see the king-
    dom of God."
4   Nicodemus said to Him, "How can a man be born when
    he is old? Can he enter a second time into his mother's
    womb and be born?"
5   Jesus answered, "Most assuredly, I say to you, unless
    one is born of water and the Spirit, he cannot enter the
    kingdom of God.
6   "That which is born of the flesh is flesh, and that which
    is born of the Spirit is spirit.
7   "Do not marvel that I said to you, 'You must be born
    again.'
8   "The wind blows where it wishes, and you hear the
    sound of it, but cannot tell where it comes from and
    where it goes. So is everyone who is born of the Spirit."
9   Nicodemus answered and said to Him, "How can these
    things be?"
10 Jesus answered and said to him, "Are you the teacher of
    Israel, and do not know these things?
11 "Most assuredly, I say to you, We speak what We know
    and testify what We have seen, and you do not receive
    Our witness.
12 "If I have told you earthly things and you do not believe,
    how will you believe if I tell you heavenly things?
13 "No one has ascended to heaven but He who came down

from heaven, that is, the Son of Man who is in heaven.

14 "And as Moses lifted up the serpent in the wilderness, even so must the Son of Man be lifted up,

15 "that whoever believes in Him should not perish but have eternal life.

16 "For God so loved the world that He gave His only begotten Son, that whoever believes in Him should not perish but have everlasting life.

17 "For God did not send His Son into the world to condemn the world, but that the world through Him might be saved.

18 "He who believes in Him is not condemned; but he who does not believe is condemned already, because he has not believed in the name of the only begotten Son of God.

19 "And this is the condemnation, that the light has come into the world, and men loved darkness rather than light, because their deeds were evil.

20 "For everyone practicing evil hates the light and does not come to the light, lest his deeds should be exposed.

21 "But he who does the truth comes to the light, that his deeds may be clearly seen, that they have been done in God."

22 After these things Jesus and His disciples came into the land of Judea, and there He remained with them and baptized.

23 Now John also was baptizing in Aenon near Salim, because there was much water there. And they came and were baptized.

24 For John had not yet been thrown into prison.

25 Then there arose a dispute between some of John's disciples and the Jews about purification.

26 And they came to John and said to him, "Rabbi, He who was with you beyond the Jordan, to whom you have testified—behold, He is baptizing, and all are coming to Him!"

27 John answered and said, "A man can receive nothing unless it has been given to him from heaven.

28 "You yourselves bear me witness, that I said, 'I am not the Christ,' but, 'I have been sent before Him.'

29 "He who has the bride is the bridegroom; but the friend of the bridegroom, who stands and hears him, rejoices greatly because of the bridegroom's voice. Therefore this joy of mine is fulfilled.

30 "He must increase, but I must decrease.

31 "He who comes from above is above all; he who is of the earth is earthly and speaks of the earth. He who comes from heaven is above all.

32 "And what He has seen and heard, that He testifies; and no one receives His testimony.

33 "He who has received His testimony has certified that God is true.

34 "For He whom God has sent speaks the words of God, for God does not give the Spirit by measure.

35 "The Father loves the Son, and has given all things into His hand.

36 "He who believes in the Son has everlasting life; and he who does not believe the Son shall not see life, but the wrath of God abides on him."

45

John 4

1 Therefore, when the Lord knew that the Pharisees had heard that Jesus made and baptized more disciples than John

2 (though Jesus Himself did not baptize, but His disciples),

3 He left Judea and departed again to Galilee.

4 But He needed to go through Samaria.

5 So He came to a city of Samaria which is called Sychar, near the plot of ground that Jacob gave to his son Joseph.

6 Now Jacob's well was there. Jesus therefore, being wearied from His journey, sat thus by the well. It was about the sixth hour.

7 A woman of Samaria came to draw water. Jesus said to her, "Give Me a drink."

8   For His disciples had gone away into the city to buy food.

9   Then the woman of Samaria said to Him, "How is it that You, being a Jew, ask a drink from me, a Samaritan woman?" For Jews have no dealings with Samaritans.

10 Jesus answered and said to her, "If you knew the gift of God, and who it is who says to you, 'Give Me a drink,' you would have asked Him, and He would have given you living water."

11 The woman said to Him, "Sir, You have nothing to draw with, and the well is deep. Where then do You get that living water?

12 "Are You greater than our father Jacob, who gave us the well, and drank from it himself, as well as his sons and his livestock?"

13 Jesus answered and said to her, "Whoever drinks of this water will thirst again,

14 "but whoever drinks of the water that I shall give him will never thirst. But the water that I shall give him will become in him a fountain of water springing up into ever-lasting life."

15 The woman said to Him, "Sir, give me this water, that I may not thirst, nor come here to draw."

16 Jesus said to her, "Go, call your husband, and come here."

17 The woman answered and said, "I have no husband." Jesus said to her, "You have well said, 'I have no husband,'

18 "for you have had five husbands, and the one whom you now have is not your husband; in that you spoke truly."

19 The woman said to Him, "Sir, I perceive that You are a prophet.

20 "Our fathers worshiped on this mountain, and you Jews say that in Jerusalem is the place where one ought to worship."

21 Jesus said to her, "Woman, believe Me, the hour is coming when you will neither on this mountain, nor in Jerusalem, worship the Father.

22 "You worship what you do not know; we know what we worship, for salvation is of the Jews.

23 "But the hour is coming, and now is, when the true worshipers will worship the Father in spirit and truth; for the Father is seeking such to worship Him.

24 "God is Spirit, and those who worship Him must worship in spirit and truth."

25 The woman said to Him, "I know that Messiah is coming" (who is called Christ). "When He comes, He will tell us all things."

26 Jesus said to her, "I who speak to you am He."

27 And at this point His disciples came, and they marveled that He talked with a woman; yet no one said, "What do You seek?" or, "Why are You talking with her?"

28 The woman then left her waterpot, went her way into the city, and said to the men,

29 "Come, see a Man who told me all things that I ever did. Could this be the Christ?"

30 Then they went out of the city and came to Him.

31 In the meantime His disciples urged Him, saying, "Rabbi, eat."

47

32 But He said to them, "I have food to eat of which you do not know."

33 Therefore the disciples said to one another, "Has anyone brought Him anything to eat?"

34 Jesus said to them, "My food is to do the will of Him who sent Me, and to finish His work.

35 "Do you not say, 'There are still four months and then comes the harvest'? Behold, I say to you, lift up your eyes and look at the fields, for they are already white for harvest!

36 "And he who reaps receives wages, and gathers fruit for eternal life, that both he who sows and he who reaps may rejoice together.

37 "For in this the saying is true: 'One sows and another reaps.'

38 "I sent you to reap that for which you have not labored; others have labored, and you have entered into their labors."

39 And many of the Samaritans of that city believed in Him

because of the word of the woman who testified, "He told me all that I ever did."

40 So when the Samaritans had come to Him, they urged Him to stay with them; and He stayed there two days.

41 And many more believed because of His own word.

42 Then they said to the woman, "Now we believe, not because of what you said, for we have heard for ourselves and know that this is indeed the Christ, the Savior of the world."

43 Now after the two days He departed from there and went to Galilee.

44 For Jesus Himself testified that a prophet has no honor in his own country.

45 So when He came to Galilee, the Galileans received Him, having seen all the things He did in Jerusalem at the feast; for they also had gone to the feast.

46 So Jesus came again to Cana of Galilee where He had made the water wine. And there was a certain nobleman whose son was sick at Capernaum.

48

47 When he heard that Jesus had come out of Judea into Galilee, he went to Him and implored Him to come down and heal his son, for he was at the point of death.

48 Then Jesus said to him, "Unless you people see signs and wonders, you will by no means believe."

49 The nobleman said to Him, "Sir, come down before my child dies!"

50 Jesus said to him, "Go your way; your son lives." So the man believed the word that Jesus spoke to him, and he went his way.

51 And as he was now going down, his servants met him and told him, saying, "Your son lives!"

52 Then he inquired of them the hour when he got better. And they said to him, "Yesterday at the seventh hour the fever left him."

53 So the father knew that it was at the same hour in which Jesus said to him, "Your son lives." And he himself believed, and his whole household.

54 This again is the second sign that Jesus did when He had come out of Judea into Galilee.

John 5

1 After this there was a feast of the Jews, and Jesus went up to Jerusalem.

2 Now there is in Jerusalem by the Sheep Gate a pool, which is called in Hebrew, Bethesda, having five porches.

3 In these lay a great multitude of sick people, blind, lame, paralyzed, waiting for the moving of the water.

4 For an angel went down at a certain time into the pool and stirred up the water; then whoever stepped in first, after the stirring of the water, was made well of whatever disease he had.

5 Now a certain man was there who had an infirmity thirty-eight years.

49

6 When Jesus saw him lying there, and knew that he already had been in that condition a long time, He said to him, "Do you want to be made well?"

7 The sick man answered Him, "Sir, I have no man to put me into the pool when the water is stirred up; but while I am coming, another steps down before me."

8 Jesus said to him, "Rise, take up your bed and walk."

9 And immediately the man was made well, took up his bed, and walked. And that day was the Sabbath.

10 The Jews therefore said to him who was cured, "It is the Sabbath; it is not lawful for you to carry your bed."

11 He answered them, "He who made me well said to me, 'Take up your bed and walk.'"

12 Then they asked him, "Who is the Man who said to you, 'Take up your bed and walk'?"

13 But the one who was healed did not know who it was, for Jesus had withdrawn, a multitude being in that place.

14 Afterward Jesus found him in the temple, and said to him, "See, you have been made well. Sin no more, lest a worse thing come upon you."

15 The man departed and told the Jews that it was Jesus who had made him well.

16 For this reason the Jews persecuted Jesus, and sought to kill Him, because He had done these things on the Sabbath.

17 But Jesus answered them, "My Father has been working until now, and I have been working."

18 Therefore the Jews sought all the more to kill Him, because He not only broke the Sabbath, but also said that God was His Father, making Himself equal with God.

19 Then Jesus answered and said to them, "Most assuredly, I say to you, the Son can do nothing of Himself, but what He sees the Father do; for whatever He does, the Son also does in like manner.

20 "For the Father loves the Son, and shows Him all things that He Himself does; and He will show Him greater works than these, that you may marvel.

50

21 "For as the Father raises the dead and gives life to them, even so the Son gives life to whom He will.

22 "For the Father judges no one, but has committed all judgment to the Son,

23 "that all should honor the Son just as they honor the Father. He who does not honor the Son does not honor the Father who sent Him.

24 "Most assuredly, I say to you, he who hears My word and believes in Him who sent Me has everlasting life, and shall not come into judgment, but has passed from death into life.

25 "Most assuredly, I say to you, the hour is coming, and now is, when the dead will hear the voice of the Son of God; and those who hear will live.

26 "For as the Father has life in Himself, so He has granted the Son to have life in Himself,

27 "and has given Him authority to execute judgment also, because He is the Son of Man.

28 "Do not marvel at this; for the hour is coming in which all who are in the graves will hear His voice

29 "and come forth—those who have done good, to the resurrection of life, and those who have done evil, to the resurrection of condemnation.

30 "I can of Myself do nothing. As I hear, I judge; and My judgment is righteous, because I do not seek My own will but the will of the Father who sent Me.

31 "If I bear witness of Myself, My witness is not true.

32 "There is another who bears witness of Me, and I know that the witness which He witnesses of Me is true.

33 "You have sent to John, and he has bore witness to the truth.

34 "Yet I do not receive testimony from man, but I say these things that you may be saved.

35 "He was the burning and shining lamp, and you were willing for a time to rejoice in his light.

36 "But I have a greater witness than John's; for the works which the Father has given Me to finish—the very works that I do—bear witness of Me, that the Father has sent Me.

51

37 "And the Father Himself, who sent Me, has testified of Me. You have neither heard His voice at any time, nor seen His form.

38 "But you do not have His word abiding in you, because whom He sent, Him you do not believe.

39 "You search the Scriptures, for in them you think you have eternal life; and these are they which testify of Me.

40 "But you are not willing to come to Me that you may have life.

41 "I do not receive honor from men.

42 "But I know you, that you do not have the love of God in you.

43 "I have come in My Father's name, and you do not receive Me; if another comes in his own name, him you will receive.

44 "How can you believe, who receive honor from one another, and do not seek the honor that comes from the only God?

45 "Do not think that I shall accuse you to the Father; there is one who accuses you—Moses, in whom you trust.

46 "For if you believed Moses, you would believe Me; for he wrote about Me.

47 "But if you do not believe his writings, how will you believe My words?"

John 6

1 After these things Jesus went over the Sea of Galilee, which is the Sea of Tiberias.

2 Then a great multitude followed Him, because they saw His signs which He performed on those who were diseased.

3 And Jesus went up on a mountain, and there He sat with His disciples.

4 Now the Passover, a feast of the Jews, was near.

5 Then Jesus lifted up His eyes, and seeing a great multitude coming toward Him, He said to Philip, "Where shall we buy bread, that these may eat?"

6 But this He said to test him, for He Himself knew what He would do.

7 Philip answered Him, "Two hundred denarii worth of bread is not sufficient for them, that every one of them may have a little."

8 One of His disciples, Andrew, Simon Peter's brother, said to Him,

9 "There is a lad here who has five barley loaves and two small fish, but what are they among so many?"

10 Then Jesus said, "Make the people sit down." Now there was much grass in the place. So the men sat down, in number about five thousand.

11 And Jesus took the loaves, and when He had given thanks He distributed them to the disciples, and the disciples to

those sitting down; and likewise of the fish, as much as they wanted.

12 So when they were filled, He said to His disciples, "Gather up the fragments that remain, so that nothing is lost."

13 Therefore they gathered them up, and filled twelve baskets with the fragments of the five barley loaves which were left over by those who had eaten.

14 Then those men, when they had seen the sign that Jesus did, said, "This is truly the Prophet who is to come into the world."

15 Therefore when Jesus perceived that they were about to come and take Him by force to make Him king, He departed again to a mountain by Himself alone.

16 And when evening came, His disciples went down to the sea,

17 got into the boat, and went over the sea toward Capernaum. And it was now dark, and Jesus had not come to them.

18 Then the sea arose because a great wind was blowing.

53

19 So when they had rowed about three or four miles, they saw Jesus walking on the sea and drawing near the boat; and they were afraid.

20 But He said to them, "It is I; do not be afraid."

21 Then they willingly received Him into the boat, and immediately the boat was at the land where they were going.

22 On the following day, when the people who were standing on the other side of the sea saw that there was no other boat there, except that one which His disciples had entered, and that Jesus had not entered the boat with His disciples, but His disciples had gone away alone—

23 however, other boats came from Tiberias, near the place where they ate bread after the Lord had given thanks—

24 when the people therefore saw that Jesus was not there, nor His disciples, they also got into boats and came to Capernaum, seeking Jesus.

25 And when they found Him on the other side of the sea, they said to Him, "Rabbi, when did You come here?"

26 Jesus answered them and said, "Most assuredly, I say to you, you seek Me, not because you saw the signs, but because you ate of the loaves and were filled.

27 "Do not labor for the food which perishes, but for the food which endures to everlasting life, which the Son of Man will give you, because God the Father has set His seal on Him."

28 Then they said to Him, "What shall we do, that we may work the works of God?"

29 Jesus answered and said to them, "This is the work of God, that you believe in Him whom He sent."

30 Therefore they said to Him, "What sign will You perform then, that we may see it and believe You? What work will You do?

31 "Our fathers ate the manna in the desert; as it is written, 'He gave them bread from heaven to eat.'"

32 Then Jesus said to them, "Most assuredly, I say to you, Moses did not give you the bread from heaven, but My Father gives you the true bread from heaven.

54

33 "For the bread of God is He who comes down from heaven and gives life to the world."

34 Then they said to Him, "Lord, give us this bread always."

35 And Jesus said to them, "I am the bread of life. He who comes to Me shall never hunger, and he who believes in Me shall never thirst.

36 "But I said to you that you have seen Me and yet do not believe.

37 "All that the Father gives Me will come to Me, and the one who comes to Me I will by no means cast out.

38 "For I have come down from heaven, not to do My own will, but the will of Him who sent Me.

39 "This is the will of the Father who sent Me, that of all He has given Me I should lose nothing, but should raise it up at the last day.

40 "And this is the will of Him who sent Me, that everyone who sees the Son and believes in Him may have everlasting life; and I will raise him up at the last day."

41 The Jews then murmured against Him, because He said, "I am the bread which came down from heaven."

42 And they said, "Is not this Jesus, the son of Joseph, whose father and mother we know? How is it then that He says, 'I have come down from heaven'?"

43 Jesus therefore answered and said to them, "Do not murmur among yourselves.

44 "No one can come to Me unless the Father who sent Me draws him; and I will raise him up at the last day.

45 "It is written in the prophets, 'And they shall all be taught by God.' Therefore everyone who has heard and learned from the Father comes to Me.

46 "Not that anyone has seen the Father, except He who is from God; He has seen the Father.

47 "Most assuredly, I say to you, he who believes in Me has everlasting life.

48 "I am the bread of life.

49 "Your fathers ate the manna in the wilderness, and are dead.

50 "This is the bread which comes down from heaven, that one may eat of it and not die.

55

51 "I am the living bread which came down from heaven. If anyone eats of this bread, he will live forever; and the bread that I shall give is My flesh, which I shall give for the life of the world."

52 The Jews therefore quarreled among themselves, saying, "How can this Man give us His flesh to eat?"

53 Then Jesus said to them, "Most assuredly, I say to you, unless you eat the flesh of the Son of Man and drink His blood, you have no life in you.

54 "Whoever eats My flesh and drinks My blood has eternal life, and I will raise him up at the last day.

55 "For My flesh is food indeed, and My blood is drink indeed.

56 "He who eats My flesh and drinks My blood abides in Me, and I in him.

57 "As the living Father sent Me, and I live because of the Father, so he who feeds on Me will live because of Me.

58 "This is the bread which came down from heaven—not as your fathers ate the manna, and are dead. He who eats this bread will live forever."

59 These things He said in the synagogue as He taught in Capernaum.

60 Therefore many of His disciples, when they heard this, said, "This is a hard saying; who can understand it?"

61 When Jesus knew in Himself that His disciples murmured about this, He said to them, "Does this offend you?

62 "What then if you should see the Son of Man ascend where He was before?

63 "It is the Spirit who gives life; the flesh profits nothing. The words that I speak to you are spirit, and they are life.

64 "But there are some of you who do not believe." For Jesus knew from the beginning who they were who did not believe, and who would betray Him.

65 And He said, "Therefore I have said to you that no one can come to Me unless it has been granted to him by My Father."

66 From that time many of His disciples went back and walked with Him no more.

67 Then Jesus said to the twelve, "Do you also want to go away?"

68 Then Simon Peter answered Him, "Lord, to whom shall we go? You have the words of eternal life.

69 "Also we have come to believe and know that You are the Christ, the Son of the living God."

70 Jesus answered them, "Did I not choose you, the twelve, and one of you is a devil?"

71 He spoke of Judas Iscariot, the son of Simon, for it was he who would betray Him, being one of the twelve.

John 7

1 After these things Jesus walked in Galilee; for He did not want to walk in Judea, because the Jews sought to kill Him.

2 Now the Jews' Feast of Tabernacles was at hand.

3 His brothers therefore said to Him, "Depart from here and go into Judea, that Your disciples also may see the works that You are doing.

4 "For no one does anything in secret while he himself seeks to be known openly. If You do these things, show Yourself to the world."

5 For even His brothers did not believe in Him.

6 Then Jesus said to them, "My time has not yet come, but your time is always ready.

7 "The world cannot hate you, but it hates Me because I testify of it that its works are evil.

8 "You go up to this feast. I am not yet going up to this feast, for My time has not yet fully come."

9 When He had said these things to them, He remained in Galilee.

10 But when His brothers had gone up, then He also went up to the feast, not openly, but as it were in secret.

11 Then the Jews sought Him at the feast, and said, "Where is He?"

12 And there was much murmuring among the people concerning Him. Some said, "He is good"; others said, "No, on the contrary, He deceives the people."

13 However, no one spoke openly of Him for fear of the Jews.

14 Now about the middle of the feast Jesus went up into the temple and taught.

15 And the Jews marveled, saying, "How does this Man know letters, having never studied?"

16 Jesus answered them and said, "My doctrine is not Mine, but His who sent Me.

57

17 "If anyone wants to do His will, he shall know concerning the doctrine, whether it is from God or whether I speak on My own authority.

18 "He who speaks from himself seeks his own glory; but He who seeks the glory of the One who sent Him is true, and no unrighteousness is in Him.

19 "Did not Moses give you the law, and yet none of you keeps the law? Why do you seek to kill Me?"

20 The people answered and said, "You have a demon. Who is seeking to kill You?"

21 Jesus answered and said to them, "I did one work, and you all marvel.

22 "Moses therefore gave you circumcision (not that it is from Moses, but from the fathers), and you circumcise a man on the Sabbath.

23 "If a man receives circumcision on the Sabbath, so that the law of Moses should not be broken, are you angry with Me because I made a man completely well on the Sabbath?

24 "Do not judge according to appearance, but judge with righteous judgment."

25 Then some of them from Jerusalem said, "Is this not He whom they seek to kill?

26 "But look! He speaks boldly, and they say nothing to Him. Do the rulers know indeed that this is truly the Christ?

27 "However, we know where this Man is from; but when the Christ comes, no one knows where He is from."

28 Then Jesus cried out, as He taught in the temple, saying, "You both know Me, and you know where I am from; and I have not come of Myself, but He who sent Me is true, whom you do not know.

29 "But I know Him, for I am from Him, and He sent Me."

30 Then they sought to take Him; but no one laid a hand on Him, because His hour had not yet come.

31 And many of the people believed in Him, and said, "When the Christ comes, will He do more signs than these which this Man has done?"

32 The Pharisees heard the crowd murmuring these things concerning Him, and the Pharisees and the chief priests sent officers to take Him.

33 Then Jesus said to them, "I shall be with you a little while longer, and then I go to Him who sent Me.

34 "You will seek Me and not find Me, and where I am you cannot come."

35 Then the Jews said among themselves, "Where does He intend to go that we shall not find Him? Does He intend to go to the Dispersion among the Greeks and teach the Greeks?

36 "What is this thing that He said, 'You will seek Me and not find Me, and where I am you cannot come'?"

37 On the last day, that great day of the feast, Jesus stood and cried out, saying, "If anyone thirsts, let him come to Me and drink.

38 "He who believes in Me, as the Scripture has said, out of his heart will flow rivers of living water."

39 But this He spoke concerning the Spirit, whom those believing in Him would receive; for the Holy Spirit was not yet given, because Jesus was not yet glorified.

40 Therefore many from the crowd, when they heard this saying, said, "Truly this is the Prophet."

41 Others said, "This is the Christ," but some said, "Will the Christ come out of Galilee?

42 "Has not the Scripture said that the Christ comes from the seed of David and from the town of Bethlehem, where David was?"

43 So there was a division among the people because of Him.

44 Now some of them wanted to take Him, but no one laid hands on Him.

45 Then the officers came to the chief priests and Pharisees, who said to them, "Why have you not brought Him?"

46 The officers answered, "No man ever spoke like this Man!"

47 Then the Pharisees answered them, "Are you also deceived?

48 "Have any of the rulers or the Pharisees believed in Him?

49 "But this crowd that does not know the law is accursed."

50 Nicodemus (he who came to Jesus by night, being one of them) said to them,

51 "Does our law judge a man before it hears him and knows what he is doing?"

52 They answered and said to him, "Are you also from Galilee? Search and look, for no prophet has arisen out of Galilee."

53 And everyone went to his own house.

John 8

♦   ♦   ♦   ♦   ♦   ♦   ♦

1 But Jesus went to the Mount of Olives.

2 But early in the morning He came again into the temple, and all the people came to Him; and He sat down and taught them.

3 Then the scribes and Pharisees brought to Him a woman caught in adultery. And when they had set her in the midst,

4 they said to Him, "Teacher, this woman was caught in adultery, in the very act.

5 "Now Moses, in the law, commanded us that such should be stoned. But what do You say?"

6 This they said, testing Him, that they might have something of which to accuse Him. But Jesus stooped down and wrote on the ground with His finger, as though He did not hear.

7 So when they continued asking Him, He raised Himself up and said to them, "He who is without sin among you, let him throw a stone at her first."

8 And again He stooped down and wrote on the ground.

9 Then those who heard it, being convicted by their conscience, went out one by one, beginning with the oldest even to the last. And Jesus was left alone, and the woman standing in the midst.

10 When Jesus had raised Himself up and saw no one but the woman, He said to her, "Woman, where are those

accusers of yours? Has no one condemned you?"

11 She said, "No one, Lord." And Jesus said to her, "Neither do I condemn you; go and sin no more."

12 Then Jesus spoke to them again, saying, "I am the light of the world. He who follows Me shall not walk in darkness, but have the light of life."

13 The Pharisees therefore said to Him, "You bear witness of Yourself; Your witness is not true."

14 Jesus answered and said to them, "Even if I bear witness of Myself, My witness is true, for I know where I came from and where I am going; but you do not know where I come from and where I am going.

15 "You judge according to the flesh; I judge no one.

16 "And yet if I do judge, My judgment is true; for I am not alone, but I am with the Father who sent Me.

17 "It is also written in your law that the testimony of two men is true.

18 "I am One who bears witness of Myself, and the Father who sent Me bears witness of Me."

19 Then they said to Him, "Where is Your Father?" Jesus answered, "You know neither Me nor My Father. If you had known Me, you would have known My Father also."

20 These words Jesus spoke in the treasury, as He taught in the temple; and no one laid hands on Him, for His hour had not yet come.

21 Then Jesus said to them again, "I am going away, and you will seek Me, and will die in your sin. Where I go you cannot come."

22 So the Jews said, "Will He kill Himself, because He says, 'Where I go you cannot come'?"

23 And He said to them, "You are from beneath; I am from above. You are of this world; I am not of this world.

24 "Therefore I said to you that you will die in your sins; for if you do not believe that I am He, you will die in your sins."

25 Then they said to Him, "Who are You?" And Jesus said to them, "Just what I have been saying to you from the beginning.

26 "I have many things to say and to judge concerning you, but He who sent Me is true; and I speak to the world those things which I heard from Him."

27 They did not understand that He spoke to them of the Father.

28 Then Jesus said to them, "When you lift up the Son of Man, then you will know that I am He, and that I do nothing of Myself; but as My Father taught Me, I speak these things.

29 "And He who sent Me is with Me. The Father has not left Me alone, for I always do those things that please Him."

30 As He spoke these words, many believed in Him.

31 Then Jesus said to those Jews who believed Him, "If you abide in My word, you are My disciples indeed.

32 "And you shall know the truth, and the truth shall make you free."

33 They answered Him, "We are Abraham's descendants, and have never been in bondage to anyone. How can you say, 'You will be made free'?"

34 Jesus answered them, "Most assuredly, I say to you, whoever commits sin is a slave of sin.

35 "And a slave does not abide in the house forever, but a son abides forever.

36 "Therefore if the Son makes you free, you shall be free indeed.

37 "I know that you are Abraham's descendants, but you seek to kill Me, because My word has no place in you.

38 "I speak what I have seen with My Father, and you do what you have seen with your father."

39 They answered and said to Him, "Abraham is our father." Jesus said to them, "If you were Abraham's children, you would do the works of Abraham.

40 "But now you seek to kill Me, a Man who has told you the truth which I heard from God. Abraham did not do this.

41 "You do the deeds of your father." Then they said to Him, "We were not born of fornication; we have one Father—God."

42 Jesus said to them, "If God were your Father, you would love Me, for I proceeded forth and came from God; nor have I come of Myself, but He sent Me.

43 "Why do you not understand My speech? Because you are not able to listen to My word.

44 "You are of your father the devil, and the desires of your father you want to do. He was a murderer from the beginning, and does not stand in the truth, because there is no truth in him. When he speaks a lie, he speaks from his own resources, for he is a liar and the father of it.

45 "But because I tell the truth, you do not believe Me.

46 "Which of you convicts Me of sin? And if I tell the truth, why do you not believe Me?

47 "He who is of God hears God's words; therefore you do not hear, because you are not of God."

48 Then the Jews answered and said to Him, "Do we not say rightly that You are a Samaritan and have a demon?"

49 Jesus answered, "I do not have a demon; but I honor My Father, and you dishonor Me.

50 "And I do not seek My own glory; there is One who seeks and judges.

51 "Most assuredly, I say to you, if anyone keeps My word he shall never see death."

52 Then the Jews said to Him, "Now we know that You have a demon! Abraham is dead, and the prophets; and You say, 'If anyone keeps My word he shall never taste death.'

53 "Are You greater than our father Abraham, who is dead? And the prophets are dead. Whom do You make Yourself out to be?"

54 Jesus answered, "If I honor Myself, My honor is nothing. It is My Father who honors Me, of whom you say that He is your God.

55 "Yet you have not known Him, but I know Him. And if I say, 'I do not know Him,' I shall be a liar like you; but I do know Him and keep His word.

56 "Your father Abraham rejoiced to see My day, and he saw it and was glad."

57 Then the Jews said to Him, "You are not yet fifty years old, and have You seen Abraham?"

58 Jesus said to them, "Most assuredly, I say to you, before Abraham was, I AM."

59 Then they took up stones to throw at Him; but Jesus hid Himself and went out of the temple, going through the midst of them, and so passed by.

John 9

❖   ❖   ❖   ❖   ❖   ❖   ❖

1 Now as Jesus passed by, He saw a man who was blind from birth.

2 And His disciples asked Him, saying, "Rabbi, who sinned, this man or his parents, that he was born blind?"

3 Jesus answered, "Neither this man nor his parents sinned, but that the works of God should be revealed in him.

4 "I must work the works of Him who sent Me while it is day; the night is coming when no one can work.

5 "As long as I am in the world, I am the light of the world."

6 When He had said these things, He spat on the ground and made clay with the saliva; and He anointed the eyes of the blind man with the clay.

7 And He said to him, "Go, wash in the pool of Siloam" (which is translated, Sent). So he went and washed, and came back seeing.

8 Therefore the neighbors and those who previously had seen that he was blind said, "Is not this he who sat and begged?"

9 Some said, "This is he." Others said, "He is like him." He said, "I am he."

10 Therefore they said to him, "How were your eyes opened?"

11 He answered and said, "A Man called Jesus made clay and anointed my eyes and said to me, 'Go to the pool of Siloam

and wash.' So I went and washed, and I received sight."

12 Then they said to him, "Where is He?" He said, "I do not know."

13 They brought him who formerly was blind to the Pharisees.

14 Now it was a Sabbath when Jesus made the clay and opened his eyes.

15 Then the Pharisees also asked him again how he had received his sight. He said to them, "He put clay on my eyes, and I washed, and I see."

16 Therefore some of the Pharisees said, "This Man is not from God, because He does not keep the Sabbath." Others said, "How can a man who is a sinner do such signs?" And there was a division among them.

17 They said to the blind man again, "What do you say about Him because He opened your eyes?" He said, "He is a prophet."

18 But the Jews did not believe concerning him, that he had been blind and received his sight, until they called the parents of him who had received his sight.

65

19 And they asked them, saying, "Is this your son, who you say was born blind? How then does he now see?"

20 His parents answered them and said, "We know that this is our son, and that he was born blind;

21 "but by what means he now sees we do not know, or who opened his eyes we do not know. He is of age; ask him. He will speak for himself."

22 His parents said these things because they feared the Jews, for the Jews had agreed already that if anyone confessed that He was Christ, he would be put out of the synagogue.

23 Therefore his parents said, "He is of age; ask him."

24 So they again called the man who was blind, and said to him, "Give God the glory! We know that this Man is a sinner."

25 He answered and said, "Whether He is a sinner or not I do not know. One thing I know: that though I was blind, now I see."

26 Then they said to him again, "What did He do to you? How did He open your eyes?"

27 He answered them, "I told you already, and you did not listen. Why do you want to hear it again? Do you also want to become His disciples?"

28 Then they reviled him and said, "You are His disciple, but we are Moses' disciples.

29 "We know that God spoke to Moses; as for this fellow, we do not know where He is from."

30 The man answered and said to them, "Why, this is a marvelous thing, that you do not know where He is from, and yet He has opened my eyes!

31 "Now we know that God does not hear sinners; but if anyone is a worshiper of God and does His will, He hears him.

32 "Since the world began it has been unheard of that anyone opened the eyes of one who was born blind.

33 "If this Man were not from God, He could do nothing."

34 They answered and said to him, "You were completely born in sins, and are you teaching us?" And they cast him out.

35 Jesus heard that they had cast him out; and when He had found him, He said to him, "Do you believe in the Son of God?"

36 He answered and said, "Who is He, Lord, that I may believe in Him?"

37 And Jesus said to him, "You have both seen Him and it is He who is talking with you."

38 Then he said, "Lord, I believe!" And he worshiped Him.

39 And Jesus said, "For judgment I have come into this world, that those who do not see may see, and that those who see may be made blind."

40 Then some of the Pharisees who were with Him heard these words, and said to Him, "Are we blind also?"

41 Jesus said to them, "If you were blind, you would have no sin; but now you say, 'We see.' Therefore your sin remains.

John 10

❖   ❖   ❖   ❖   ❖   ❖   ❖

1   "Most assuredly, I say to you, he who does not enter the sheepfold by the door, but climbs up some other way, the same is a thief and a robber.

2   "But he who enters by the door is the shepherd of the sheep.

3   "To him the doorkeeper opens, and the sheep hear his voice; and he calls his own sheep by name and leads them out.

4   "And when he brings out his own sheep, he goes before them; and the sheep follow him, for they know his voice.

5   "Yet they will by no means follow a stranger, but will flee from him, for they do not know the voice of strangers."

6   Jesus used this illustration, but they did not understand the things which He spoke to them.

7   Then Jesus said to them again, "Most assuredly, I say to you, I am the door of the sheep.

8   "All who ever came before Me are thieves and robbers, but the sheep did not hear them.

9   "I am the door. If anyone enters by Me, he will be saved, and will go in and out and find pasture.

10 "The thief does not come except to steal, and to kill, and to destroy. I have come that they may have life, and that they may have it more abundantly.

11 "I am the good shepherd. The good shepherd gives His life for the sheep.

12 "But he who is a hireling and not the shepherd, one who does not own the sheep, sees the wolf coming and leaves the sheep and flees; and the wolf catches the sheep and scatters them.

13 "The hireling flees because he is a hireling and does not care about the sheep.

14 "I am the good shepherd; and I know My sheep, and am known by My own.

15 "As the Father knows Me, even so I know the Father; and I lay down My life for the sheep.

16 "And other sheep I have which are not of this fold; them also I must bring, and they will hear My voice; and there will be one flock and one shepherd.

17 "Therefore My Father loves Me, because I lay down My life that I may take it again.

18 "No one takes it from Me, but I lay it down of Myself. I have power to lay it down, and I have power to take it again. This command I have received from My Father."

19 Therefore there was a division again among the Jews because of these sayings.

20 And many of them said, "He has a demon and is mad. Why do you listen to Him?"

21 Others said, "These are not the words of one who has a demon. Can a demon open the eyes of the blind?"

22 Now it was the Feast of Dedication in Jerusalem, and it was winter.

68 ▶ 23 And Jesus walked in the temple, in Solomon's porch.

24 Then the Jews surrounded Him and said to Him, "How long do You keep us in doubt? If You are the Christ, tell us plainly."

25 Jesus answered them, "I told you, and you do not believe. The works that I do in My Father's name, they bear witness of Me.

26 "But you do not believe, because you are not of My sheep, as I said to you.

27 "My sheep hear My voice, and I know them, and they follow Me.

28 "And I give them eternal life, and they shall never perish; neither shall anyone snatch them out of My hand.

29 "My Father, who has given them to Me, is greater than all; and no one is able to snatch them out of My Father's hand.

30 "I and My Father are one."

31 Then the Jews took up stones again to stone Him.

32 Jesus answered them, "Many good works I have shown you from My Father. For which of those works do you stone Me?"

33 The Jews answered Him, saying, "For a good work we do not stone You, but for blasphemy, and because You, being a Man, make Yourself God."

34 Jesus answered them, "Is it not written in your law, 'I said, "You are gods"'?

35 "If He called them gods, to whom the word of God came (and the Scripture cannot be broken),

36 "do you say of Him whom the Father sanctified and sent into the world, 'You are blaspheming,' because I said, 'I am the Son of God'?

37 "If I do not do the works of My Father, do not believe Me;

38 "but if I do, though you do not believe Me, believe the works, that you may know and believe that the Father is in Me, and I in Him."

39 Therefore they sought again to seize Him, but He escaped out of their hand.

40 And He went away again beyond the Jordan to the place where John was baptizing at first, and there He stayed.

41 Then many came to Him and said, "John performed no sign, but all the things that John spoke about this Man were true."

42 And many believed in Him there.

John 11

❖ ❖ ❖ ❖ ❖ ❖ ❖

1 Now a certain man was sick, Lazarus of Bethany, the town of Mary and her sister Martha.

2 It was that Mary who anointed the Lord with fragrant oil and wiped His feet with her hair, whose brother Lazarus was sick.

3 Therefore the sisters sent to Him, saying, "Lord, behold, he whom You love is sick."

4 When Jesus heard that, He said, "This sickness is not unto death, but for the glory of God, that the Son of God may be glorified through it."

5   Now Jesus loved Martha and her sister and Lazarus.

6   So, when He heard that he was sick, He stayed two more days in the place where He was.

7   Then after this He said to the disciples, "Let us go to Judea again."

8   The disciples said to Him, "Rabbi, lately the Jews sought to stone You, and are You going there again?"

9   Jesus answered, "Are there not twelve hours in the day? If anyone walks in the day, he does not stumble, because he sees the light of this world.

10 "But if one walks in the night, he stumbles, because the light is not in him."

11 These things He said, and after that He said to them, "Our friend Lazarus sleeps, but I go that I may wake him up."

12 Then His disciples said, "Lord, if he sleeps he will get well."

13 However, Jesus spoke of his death, but they thought that He was speaking about taking rest in sleep.

14 Then Jesus said to them plainly, "Lazarus is dead.

15 "And I am glad for your sakes that I was not there, that you may believe. Nevertheless let us go to him."

16 Then Thomas, who is called Didymus, said to his fellow disciples, "Let us also go, that we may die with Him."

17 So when Jesus came, He found that he had already been in the tomb four days.

18 Now Bethany was near Jerusalem, about two miles away.

19 And many of the Jews had joined the women around Martha and Mary, to comfort them concerning their brother.

20 Then Martha, as soon as she heard that Jesus was coming, went and met Him, but Mary was sitting in the house.

21 Then Martha said to Jesus, "Lord, if You had been here, my brother would not have died.

22 "But even now I know that whatever You ask of God, God will give You."

23 Jesus said to her, "Your brother will rise again."

24 Martha said to Him, "I know that he will rise again in the resurrection at the last day."

25 Jesus said to her, "I am the resurrection and the life. He who believes in Me, though he may die, he shall live.

26 "And whoever lives and believes in Me shall never die. Do you believe this?"

27 She said to Him, "Yes, Lord, I believe that You are the Christ, the Son of God, who is to come into the world."

28 And when she had said these things, she went her way and secretly called Mary her sister, saying, "The Teacher has come and is calling for you."

29 As soon as she heard that, she arose quickly and came to Him.

30 Now Jesus had not yet come into the town, but was in the place where Martha met Him.

31 Then the Jews who were with her in the house, and comforting her, when they saw that Mary rose up quickly and went out, followed her, saying, "She is going to the tomb to weep there."

32 Then, when Mary came where Jesus was, and saw Him, she fell down at His feet, saying to Him, "Lord, if You had been here, my brother would not have died."

33 Therefore, when Jesus saw her weeping, and the Jews who came with her weeping, He groaned in the spirit and was troubled.

34 And He said, "Where have you laid him?" They said to Him, "Lord, come and see."

35 Jesus wept.

36 Then the Jews said, "See how He loved him!"

37 And some of them said, "Could not this Man, who opened the eyes of the blind, also have kept this man from dying?"

38 Then Jesus, again groaning in Himself, came to the tomb. It was a cave, and a stone lay against it.

39 Jesus said, "Take away the stone." Martha, the sister of him who was dead, said to Him, "Lord, by this time there is a stench, for he has been dead four days."

40 Jesus said to her, "Did I not say to you that if you would believe you would see the glory of God?"

41 Then they took away the stone from the place where the dead man was lying. And Jesus lifted up His eyes and said, "Father, I thank You that You have heard Me.

42 "And I know that You always hear Me, but because of the people who are standing by I said this, that they may believe that You sent Me."

43 Now when He had said these things, He cried with a loud voice, "Lazarus, come forth!"

44 And he who had died came out bound hand and foot with graveclothes, and his face was wrapped with a cloth. Jesus said to them, "Loose him, and let him go."

45 Then many of the Jews who had come to Mary, and had seen the things Jesus did, believed in Him.

46 But some of them went away to the Pharisees and told them the things Jesus did.

47 Then the chief priests and the Pharisees gathered a council and said, "What shall we do? For this Man works many signs.

 48 "If we let Him alone like this, everyone will believe in Him, and the Romans will come and take away both our place and nation."

49 And one of them, Caiaphas, being high priest that year, said to them, "You know nothing at all,

50 "nor do you consider that it is expedient for us that one man should die for the people, and not that the whole nation should perish."

51 Now this he did not say on his own authority; but being high priest that year he prophesied that Jesus would die for the nation,

52 and not for that nation only, but also that He would gather together in one the children of God who were scattered abroad.

53 Then from that day on they plotted to put Him to death.

54 Therefore Jesus no longer walked openly among the Jews, but went from there into the country near the wilderness, to a city called Ephraim, and there remained with His disciples.

55 And the Passover of the Jews was near, and many went from the country up to Jerusalem before the Passover, to purify themselves.

56 Then they sought Jesus, and spoke among themselves as they stood in the temple, "What do you think—that He will not come to the feast?"

57 Now both the chief priests and the Pharisees had given a command, that if anyone knew where He was, he should report it, that they might seize Him.

John 12

❖   ❖   ❖   ❖   ❖   ❖   ❖

1 Then, six days before the Passover, Jesus came to Bethany, where Lazarus was who had been dead, whom He had raised from the dead.

2 There they made Him a supper; and Martha served, but Lazarus was one of those who sat at the table with Him.

3 Then Mary took a pound of very costly oil of spikenard, anointed the feet of Jesus, and wiped His feet with her hair. And the house was filled with the fragrance of the oil.

4 Then one of His disciples, Judas Iscariot, Simon's son, who would betray Him, said,

5 "Why was this fragrant oil not sold for three hundred denarii and given to the poor?"

6 This he said, not that he cared for the poor, but because he was a thief, and had the money box; and he used to take what was put in it.

7 Then Jesus said, "Let her alone; she has kept this for the day of My burial.

8 "For the poor you have with you always, but Me you do not have always."

9 Then a great many of the Jews knew that He was there; and they came, not for Jesus' sake only, but that they might also see Lazarus, whom He had raised from the dead.

73

10 But the chief priests took counsel that they might also put Lazarus to death,

11 because on account of him many of the Jews went away and believed in Jesus.

12 The next day a great multitude that had come to the feast, when they heard that Jesus was coming to Jerusalem,

13 took branches of palm trees and went out to meet Him, and cried out: "Hosanna! 'Blessed is He who comes in the name of the Lord!' The King of Israel!"

14 Then Jesus, when He had found a young donkey, sat on it; as it is written:

15 "Fear not, daughter of Zion; behold, your King is coming, sitting on a donkey's colt."

16 His disciples did not understand these things at first; but when Jesus was glorified, then they remembered that these things were written about Him and that they had done these things to Him.

74

17 Therefore the people, who were with Him when He called Lazarus out of his tomb and raised him from the dead, bore witness.

18 For this reason the people also met Him, because they heard that He had done this sign.

19 The Pharisees therefore said among themselves, "You see that you are accomplishing nothing. Look, the world has gone after Him!"

20 Now there were certain Greeks among those who came up to worship at the feast.

21 Then they came to Philip, who was from Bethsaida of Galilee, and asked him, saying, "Sir, we wish to see Jesus."

22 Philip came and told Andrew, and in turn Andrew and Philip told Jesus.

23 But Jesus answered them, saying, "The hour has come that the Son of Man should be glorified.

24 "Most assuredly, I say to you, unless a grain of wheat falls into the ground and dies, it remains alone; but if it dies, it produces much grain.

25 "He who loves his life will lose it, and he who hates his life in this world will keep it for eternal life.

26 "If anyone serves Me, let him follow Me; and where I am, there My servant will be also. If anyone serves Me, him My Father will honor.

27 "Now My soul is troubled, and what shall I say? 'Father, save Me from this hour'? But for this purpose I came to this hour.

28 "Father, glorify Your name." Then a voice came from heaven, saying, "I have both glorified it and will glorify it again."

29 Therefore the people who stood by and heard it said that it had thundered. Others said, "An angel has spoken to Him."

30 Jesus answered and said, "This voice did not come because of Me, but for your sake.

31 "Now is the judgment of this world; now the ruler of this world will be cast out.

32 "And I, if I am lifted up from the earth, will draw all peoples to Myself."

33 This He said, signifying by what death He would die.

34 The people answered Him, "We have heard from the law that the Christ remains forever; and how can You say, 'The Son of Man must be lifted up'? Who is this Son of Man?"

75

35 Then Jesus said to them, "A little while longer the light is with you. Walk while you have the light, lest darkness overtake you; he who walks in darkness does not know where he is going.

36 "While you have the light, believe in the light, that you may become sons of light." These things Jesus spoke, and departed, and was hidden from them.

37 But although He had done so many signs before them, they did not believe in Him,

38 that the word of Isaiah the prophet might be fulfilled, which he spoke: "Lord, who has believed our report? And to whom has the arm of the LORD been revealed?"

39 Therefore they could not believe, because Isaiah said again:

40 "He has blinded their eyes and hardened their heart, lest they should see with their eyes and understand with their heart, lest they should turn, so that I should heal them."

41 These things Isaiah said when he saw His glory and spoke of Him.

42 Nevertheless even among the rulers many believed in Him, but because of the Pharisees they did not confess Him, lest they should be put out of the synagogue;

43 for they loved the praise of men more than the praise of God.

44 Then Jesus cried out and said, "He who believes in Me, believes not in Me but in Him who sent Me.

45 "And he who sees Me sees Him who sent Me.

46 "I have come as a light into the world, that whoever believes in Me should not abide in darkness.

47 "And if anyone hears My words and does not believe, I do not judge him; for I did not come to judge the world but to save the world.

48 "He who rejects Me, and does not receive My words, has that which judges him—the word that I have spoken will judge him in the last day.

49 "For I have not spoken on My own authority; but the Father who sent Me gave Me a command, what I should say and what I should speak.

50 "And I know that His command is everlasting life. Therefore, whatever I speak, just as the Father has told Me, so I speak."

John 13

1 Now before the feast of the Passover, when Jesus knew that His hour had come that He should depart from this world to the Father, having loved His own who were in the world, He loved them to the end.

2 And supper being ended, the devil having already put it into the heart of Judas Iscariot, Simon's son, to betray Him,

3 Jesus, knowing that the Father had given all things into

His hands, and that He had come from God and was going to God,

4 rose from supper and laid aside His garments, took a towel and girded Himself.

5 After that, He poured water into a basin and began to wash the disciples' feet, and to wipe them with the towel with which He was girded.

6 Then He came to Simon Peter. And Peter said to Him, "Lord, are You washing my feet?"

7 Jesus answered and said to him, "What I am doing you do not understand now, but you will know after this."

8 Peter said to Him, "You shall never wash my feet!" Jesus answered him, "If I do not wash you, you have no part with Me."

9 Simon Peter said to Him, "Lord, not my feet only, but also my hands and my head!"

10 Jesus said to him, "He who is bathed needs only to wash his feet, but is completely clean; and you are clean, but not all of you."

11 For He knew who would betray Him; therefore He said, "You are not all clean."

12 So when He had washed their feet, taken His garments, and sat down again, He said to them, "Do you know what I have done to you?

13 "You call me Teacher and Lord, and you say well, for so I am.

14 "If I then, your Lord and Teacher, have washed your feet, you also ought to wash one another's feet.

15 "For I have given you an example, that you should do as I have done to you.

16 "Most assuredly, I say to you, a servant is not greater than his master; nor is he who is sent greater than he who sent him.

17 "If you know these things, happy are you if you do them.

18 "I do not speak concerning all of you. I know whom I have chosen; but that the Scripture may be fulfilled, 'He who eats bread with Me has lifted up his heel against Me.'

19 "Now I tell you before it comes, that when it does come to pass, you may believe that I am He.

20 "Most assuredly, I say to you, he who receives whomever I send receives Me; and he who receives Me receives Him who sent Me."

21 When Jesus had said these things, He was troubled in spirit, and testified and said, "Most assuredly, I say to you, one of you will betray Me."

22 Then the disciples looked at one another, perplexed about whom He spoke.

23 Now there was leaning on Jesus' bosom one of His disciples, whom Jesus loved.

24 Simon Peter therefore motioned to him to ask who it was of whom He spoke.

25 Then, leaning back on Jesus' breast, he said to Him, "Lord, who is it?"

26 Jesus answered, "It is he to whom I shall give a piece of bread when I have dipped it." And having dipped the bread, He gave it to Judas Iscariot, the son of Simon.

27 Now after the piece of bread, Satan entered him. Then Jesus said to him, "What you do, do quickly."

28 But no one at the table knew for what reason He said this to him.

29 For some thought, because Judas had the money box, that Jesus had said to him, "Buy those things we need for the feast," or that he should give something to the poor.

30 Having received the piece of bread, he then went out immediately. And it was night.

31 So, when he had gone out, Jesus said, "Now the Son of Man is glorified, and God is glorified in Him.

32 "If God is glorified in Him, God will also glorify Him in Himself, and glorify Him immediately.

33 "Little children, I shall be with you a little while longer. You will seek Me; and as I said to the Jews, 'Where I am going, you cannot come,' so now I say to you.

34 "A new commandment I give to you, that you love one another; as I have loved you, that you also love one another.

35 "By this all will know that you are My disciples, if you have love for one another."

36 Simon Peter said to Him, "Lord, where are You going?" Jesus answered him, "Where I am going you cannot follow Me now, but you shall follow Me afterward."

37 Peter said to Him, "Lord, why can I not follow You now? I will lay down my life for Your sake."

38 Jesus answered him, "Will you lay down your life for My sake? Most assuredly, I say to you, the rooster shall not crow till you have denied Me three times.

John 14

1 "Let not your heart be troubled; you believe in God, believe also in Me.

2 "In My Father's house are many mansions; if it were not so, I would have told you. I go to prepare a place for you.

3 "And if I go and prepare a place for you, I will come again and receive you to Myself; that where I am, there you may be also.

4 "And where I go you know, and the way you know."

5 Thomas said to Him, "Lord, we do not know where You are going, and how can we know the way?"

6 Jesus said to him, "I am the way, the truth, and the life. No one comes to the Father except through Me.

7 "If you had known Me, you would have known My Father also; and from now on you know Him and have seen Him."

8 Philip said to Him, "Lord, show us the Father, and it is sufficient for us."

9 Jesus said to him, "Have I been with you so long, and yet you have not known Me, Philip? He who has seen Me has seen the Father; so how can you say, 'Show us the Father'?

10 "Do you not believe that I am in the Father, and the Father in Me? The words that I speak to you I do not speak on My own authority; but the Father who dwells in Me does the works.

11 "Believe Me that I am in the Father and the Father in Me, or else believe Me for the sake of the works themselves.

12 "Most assuredly, I say to you, he who believes in Me, the works that I do he will do also; and greater works than these he will do, because I go to My Father.

13 "And whatever you ask in My name, that I will do, that the Father may be glorified in the Son.

14 "If you ask anything in My name, I will do it.

15 "If you love Me, keep My commandments.

16 "And I will pray the Father, and He will give you another Helper, that He may abide with you forever,

17 "even the Spirit of truth, whom the world cannot receive, because it neither sees Him nor knows Him; but you know Him, for He dwells with you and will be in you.

18 "I will not leave you orphans; I will come to you.

19 "A little while longer and the world will see Me no more, but you will see Me. Because I live, you will live also.

20 "At that day you will know that I am in My Father, and you in Me, and I in you.

21 "He who has My commandments and keeps them, it is he who loves Me. And he who loves Me will be loved by My Father, and I will love him and manifest Myself to him."

22 Judas (not Iscariot) said to Him, "Lord, how is it that You will manifest Yourself to us, and not to the world?"

23 Jesus answered and said to him, "If anyone loves Me, he will keep My word; and My Father will love him, and We will come to him and make Our home with him.

24 "He who does not love Me does not keep My words; and the word which you hear is not Mine but the Father's who sent Me.

25 "These things I have spoken to you while being present with you.

26 "But the Helper, the Holy Spirit, whom the Father will send in My name, He will teach you all things, and bring to your remembrance all things that I said to you.

27 "Peace I leave with you, My peace I give to you; not as the world gives do I give to you. Let not your heart be troubled, neither let it be afraid.

28 "You have heard Me say to you, 'I am going away and coming back to you.' If you loved Me, you would rejoice because I said, 'I am going to the Father,' for My Father is greater than I.

29 "And now I have told you before it comes, that when it does come to pass, you may believe.

30 "I will no longer talk much with you, for the ruler of this world is coming, and he has nothing in Me.

31 "But that the world may know that I love the Father, and as the Father gave Me commandment, so I do. Arise, let us go from here.

John 15

81

1 "I am the true vine, and My Father is the vinedresser.

2 "Every branch in Me that does not bear fruit He takes away; and every branch that bears fruit He prunes, that it may bear more fruit.

3 "You are already clean because of the word which I have spoken to you.

4 "Abide in Me, and I in you. As the branch cannot bear fruit of itself, unless it abides in the vine, neither can you, unless you abide in Me.

5 "I am the vine, you are the branches. He who abides in Me, and I in him, bears much fruit; for without Me you can do nothing.

6 "If anyone does not abide in Me, he is cast out as a branch and is withered; and they gather them and throw

them into the fire, and they are burned.

7 "If you abide in Me, and My words abide in you, you will ask what you desire, and it shall be done for you.

8 "By this My Father is glorified, that you bear much fruit; so you will be My disciples.

9 "As the Father loved Me, I also have loved you; abide in My love.

10 "If you keep My commandments, you will abide in My love, just as I have kept My Father's commandments and abide in His love.

11 "These things I have spoken to you, that My joy may remain in you, and that your joy may be full.

12 "This is My commandment, that you love one another as I have loved you.

13 "Greater love has no one than this, than to lay down one's life for his friends.

14 "You are My friends if you do whatever I command you.

15 "No longer do I call you servants, for a servant does not know what his master is doing; but I have called you friends, for all things that I heard from My Father I have made known to you.

16 "You did not choose Me, but I chose you and appointed you that you should go and bear fruit, and that your fruit should remain, that whatever you ask the Father in My name He may give you.

17 "These things I command you, that you love one another.

18 "If the world hates you, you know that it hated Me before it hated you.

19 "If you were of the world, the world would love its own. Yet because you are not of the world, but I chose you out of the world, therefore the world hates you.

20 "Remember the word that I said to you, 'A servant is not greater than his master.' If they persecuted Me, they will also persecute you. If they kept My word, they will keep yours also.

21 "But all these things they will do to you for My name's sake, because they do not know Him who sent Me.

22 "If I had not come and spoken to them, they would have no sin, but now they have no excuse for their sin.

23 "He who hates Me hates My Father also.

24 "If I had not done among them the works which no one else did, they would have no sin; but now they have seen and also hated both Me and My Father.

25 "But this happened that the word might be fulfilled which is written in their law, 'They hated Me without a cause.'

26 "But when the Helper comes, whom I shall send to you from the Father, the Spirit of truth who proceeds from the Father, He will testify of Me.

27 "And you also will bear witness, because you have been with Me from the beginning.

John 16

❖   ❖   ❖   ❖   ❖   ❖   ❖   83

1 "These things I have spoken to you, that you should not be made to stumble.

2 "They will put you out of the synagogues; yes, the time is coming that whoever kills you will think that he offers God service.

3 "And these things they will do to you because they have not known the Father nor Me.

4 "But these things I have told you, that when the time comes, you may remember that I told you of them. And these things I did not say to you at the beginning, because I was with you.

5 "But now I go away to Him who sent Me, and none of you asks Me, 'Where are You going?'

6 "But because I have said these things to you, sorrow has filled your heart.

7 "Nevertheless I tell you the truth. It is to your advantage that I go away; for if I do not go away, the Helper will not

come to you; but if I depart, I will send Him to you.

8 "And when He has come, He will convict the world of sin, and of righteousness, and of judgment:

9 "of sin, because they do not believe in Me;

10 "of righteousness, because I go to My Father and you see Me no more;

11 "of judgment, because the ruler of this world is judged.

12 "I still have many things to say to you, but you cannot bear them now.

13 "However, when He, the Spirit of truth, has come, He will guide you into all truth; for He will not speak on His own authority, but whatever He hears He will speak; and He will tell you things to come.

14 "He will glorify Me, for He will take of what is Mine and declare it to you.

15 "All things that the Father has are Mine. Therefore I said that He will take of Mine and declare it to you.

16 "A little while, and you will not see Me; and again a little while, and you will see Me, because I go to the Father."

17 Then some of His disciples said among themselves, "What is this that He says to us, 'A little while, and you will not see Me; and again a little while, and you will see Me'; and, 'because I go to the Father'?"

18 They said therefore, "What is this that He says, 'A little while'? We do not know what He is saying."

19 Now Jesus knew that they desired to ask Him, and He said to them, "Are you inquiring among yourselves about what I said, 'A little while, and you will not see Me; and again a little while, and you will see Me'?

20 "Most assuredly, I say to you that you will weep and lament, but the world will rejoice; and you will be sorrowful, but your sorrow will be turned into joy.

21 "A woman, when she is in labor, has sorrow because her hour has come; but as soon as she has given birth to the child, she no longer remembers the anguish, for joy that a human being has been born into the world.

22 "Therefore you now have sorrow; but I will see you again

and your heart will rejoice, and your joy no one will take from you.

23 "And in that day you will ask Me nothing. Most assuredly, I say to you, whatever you ask the Father in My name He will give you.

24 "Until now you have asked nothing in My name. Ask, and you will receive, that your joy may be full.

25 "These things I have spoken to you in figurative language; but the time is coming when I will no longer speak to you in figurative language, but I will tell you plainly about the Father.

26 "In that day you will ask in My name, and I do not say to you that I shall pray the Father for you;

27 "for the Father Himself loves you, because you have loved Me, and have believed that I came forth from God.

28 "I came forth from the Father and have come into the world. Again, I leave the world and go to the Father."

29 His disciples said to Him, "See, now You are speaking plainly, and using no figure of speech!

85

30 "Now we are sure that You know all things, and have no need that anyone should question You. By this we believe that You came forth from God."

31 Jesus answered them, "Do you now believe?

32 "Indeed the hour is coming, yes, has now come, that you will be scattered, each to his own, and will leave Me alone. And yet I am not alone, because the Father is with Me.

33 "These things I have spoken to you, that in Me you may have peace. In the world you will have tribulation; but be of good cheer, I have overcome the world."

John 17

1 Jesus spoke these words, lifted up His eyes to heaven, and said: "Father, the hour has come. Glorify Your Son, that Your Son also may glorify You,

2 "as You have given Him authority over all flesh, that He should give eternal life to as many as You have given Him.

3 "And this is eternal life, that they may know You, the only true God, and Jesus Christ whom You have sent.

4 "I have glorified You on the earth. I have finished the work which You have given Me to do.

5 "And now, O Father, glorify Me together with Yourself, with the glory which I had with You before the world was.

6 "I have manifested Your name to the men whom You have given Me out of the world. They were Yours, You gave them to Me, and they have kept Your word.

7 "Now they have known that all things which You have given Me are from You.

8 "For I have given to them the words which You have given Me; and they have received them, and have known surely that I came forth from You; and they have believed that You sent Me.

9 "I pray for them. I do not pray for the world but for those whom You have given Me, for they are Yours.

10 "And all Mine are Yours, and Yours are Mine, and I am glorified in them.

11 "Now I am no longer in the world, but these are in the world, and I come to You. Holy Father, keep through Your name those whom You have given Me, that they may be one as We are.

12 "While I was with them in the world, I kept them in Your name. Those whom You gave Me I have kept; and none of them is lost except the son of perdition, that the Scripture might be fulfilled.

13 "But now I come to You, and these things I speak in the world, that they may have My joy fulfilled in themselves.

14 "I have given them Your word; and the world has hated them because they are not of the world, just as I am not of the world.

15 "I do not pray that You should take them out of the world, but that You should keep them from the evil one.

16 "They are not of the world, just as I am not of the world.

17 "Sanctify them by Your truth. Your word is truth.

18 "As You sent Me into the world, I also have sent them into the world.

19 "And for their sakes I sanctify Myself, that they also may be sanctified by the truth.

20 "I do not pray for these alone, but also for those who will believe in Me through their word;

21 "that they all may be one, as You, Father, are in Me, and I in You; that they also may be one in Us, that the world may believe that You sent Me.

22 "And the glory which You gave Me I have given them, that they may be one just as We are one:

87

23 "I in them, and You in Me; that they may be made perfect in one, and that the world may know that You have sent Me, and have loved them as You have loved Me.

24 "Father, I desire that they also whom You gave Me may be with Me where I am, that they may behold My glory which You have given Me; for You loved Me before the foundation of the world.

25 "O righteous Father! The world has not known You, but I have known You; and these have known that You sent Me.

26 "And I have declared to them Your name, and will declare it, that the love with which You loved Me may be in them, and I in them."

John 18

1   When Jesus had spoken these words, He went out with His disciples over the Brook Kidron, where there was a garden, which He and His disciples entered.

2   And Judas, who betrayed Him, also knew the place; for Jesus often met there with His disciples.

3   Then Judas, having received a detachment of troops, and officers from the chief priests and Pharisees, came there with lanterns, torches, and weapons.

4   Jesus therefore, knowing all things that would come upon Him, went forward and said to them, "Whom are you seeking?"

5   They answered Him, "Jesus of Nazareth." Jesus said to them, "I am He." And Judas, who betrayed Him, also stood with them.

6   Then—when He said to them, "I am He,"—they drew back and fell to the ground.

7   Then He asked them again, "Whom are you seeking?" And they said, "Jesus of Nazareth."

8   Jesus answered, "I have told you that I am He. Therefore, if you seek Me, let these go their way,"

9   that the saying might be fulfilled which He spoke, "Of those whom You gave Me I have lost none."

10   Then Simon Peter, having a sword, drew it and struck the high priest's servant, and cut off his right ear. The servant's name was Malchus.

11   Then Jesus said to Peter, "Put your sword into the sheath. Shall I not drink the cup which My Father has given Me?"

12   Then the detachment of troops and the captain and the officers of the Jews arrested Jesus and bound Him.

13   And they led Him away to Annas first, for he was the father-in-law of Caiaphas who was high priest that year.

14 Now it was Caiaphas who gave counsel to the Jews that it was expedient that one man should die for the people.

15 And Simon Peter followed Jesus, and so did another disciple. Now that disciple was known to the high priest, and went with Jesus into the courtyard of the high priest.

16 But Peter stood at the door outside. Then the other disciple, who was known to the high priest, went out and spoke to her who kept the door, and brought Peter in.

17 Then the servant girl who kept the door said to Peter, "You are not also one of this Man's disciples, are you?" He said, "I am not."

18 And the servants and officers who had made a fire of coals stood there, for it was cold, and they warmed themselves. And Peter stood with them and warmed himself.

19 The high priest then asked Jesus about His disciples and His doctrine.

20 Jesus answered him, "I spoke openly to the world. I always taught in synagogues and in the temple, where the Jews always meet, and in secret I have said nothing.

21 "Why do you ask Me? Ask those who have heard Me what I said to them. Indeed they know what I said."

22 And when He had said these things, one of the officers who stood by struck Jesus with the palm of his hand, saying, "Do You answer the high priest like that?"

23 Jesus answered him, "If I have spoken evil, bear witness of the evil; but if well, why do you strike Me?"

24 Then Annas sent Him bound to Caiaphas the high priest.

25 Now Simon Peter stood and warmed himself. Therefore they said to him, "You are not also one of His disciples, are you?" He denied it and said, "I am not!"

26 One of the servants of the high priest, a relative of him whose ear Peter cut off, said, "Did I not see you in the garden with Him?"

27 Peter then denied again; and immediately a rooster crowed.

28 Then they led Jesus from Caiaphas to the Praetorium, and it was early morning. But they themselves did not go

into the Praetorium, lest they should be defiled, but that they might eat the Passover.

29 Pilate then went out to them and said, "What accusation do you bring against this Man?"

30 They answered and said to him, "If He were not an evil-doer, we would not have delivered Him up to you."

31 Then Pilate said to them, "You take Him and judge Him according to your law." Therefore the Jews said to him, "It is not lawful for us to put anyone to death,"

32 that the saying of Jesus might be fulfilled which He spoke, signifying by what death He would die.

33 Then Pilate entered the Praetorium again, called Jesus, and said to Him, "Are You the King of the Jews?"

34 Jesus answered him, "Are you speaking for yourself on this, or did others tell you this about Me?"

35 Pilate answered, "Am I a Jew? Your own nation and the chief priests have delivered You to me. What have You done?"

36 Jesus answered, "My kingdom is not of this world. If My kingdom were of this world, My servants would fight, so that I should not be delivered to the Jews; but now My kingdom is not from here."

37 Pilate therefore said to Him, "Are You a king then?" Jesus answered, "You say rightly that I am a king. For this cause I was born, and for this cause I have come into the world, that I should bear witness to the truth. Everyone who is of the truth hears My voice."

38 Pilate said to Him, "What is truth?" And when he had said this, he went out again to the Jews, and said to them, "I find no fault in Him at all.

39 "But you have a custom that I should release someone to you at the Passover. Do you therefore want me to release to you the King of the Jews?"

40 Then they all cried again, saying, "Not this Man, but Barabbas!" Now Barabbas was a robber.

John 19

1 So then Pilate took Jesus and scourged Him.

2 And the soldiers twisted a crown of thorns and put it on His head, and they put on Him a purple robe.

3 Then they said, "Hail, King of the Jews!" And they struck Him with their hands.

4 Pilate then went out again, and said to them, "Behold, I am bringing Him out to you, that you may know that I find no fault in Him."

5 Then Jesus came out, wearing the crown of thorns and the purple robe. And Pilate said to them, "Behold the Man!"

6 Therefore, when the chief priests and officers saw Him, they cried out, saying, "Crucify Him, crucify Him!" Pilate said to them, "You take Him and crucify Him, for I find no fault in Him."

7 The Jews answered him, "We have a law, and according to our law He ought to die, because He made Himself the Son of God."

8 Therefore, when Pilate heard that saying, he was the more afraid,

9 and went again into the Praetorium, and said to Jesus, "Where are You from?" But Jesus gave him no answer.

10 Then Pilate said to Him, "Are You not speaking to me? Do You not know that I have power to crucify You, and power to release You?"

11 Jesus answered, "You could have no power at all against Me unless it had been given you from above. Therefore the one who delivered Me to you has the greater sin."

12 From then on Pilate sought to release Him, but the Jews cried out, saying, "If you let this Man go, you are not Caesar's friend. Whoever makes himself a king speaks against Caesar."

13 When Pilate therefore heard that saying, he brought

Jesus out and sat down in the judgment seat in a place that is called The Pavement, but in Hebrew, Gabbatha.

14 Now it was the Preparation Day of the Passover, and about the sixth hour. And he said to the Jews, "Behold your King!"

15 But they cried out, "Away with Him, away with Him! Crucify Him!" Pilate said to them, "Shall I crucify your King?" The chief priests answered, "We have no king but Caesar!"

16 So he delivered Him to them to be crucified. So they took Jesus and led Him away.

17 And He, bearing His cross, went out to a place called the Place of a Skull, which is called in Hebrew, Golgotha,

18 where they crucified Him, and two others with Him, one on either side, and Jesus in the center.

19 Now Pilate wrote a title and put it on the cross. And the writing was: JESUS OF NAZARETH, THE KING OF THE JEWS.

20 Then many of the Jews read this title, for the place where Jesus was crucified was near the city; and it was written in Hebrew, Greek, and Latin.

21 Then the chief priests of the Jews said to Pilate, "Do not write, 'The King of the Jews,' but, 'He said, "I am the King of the Jews."' "

22 Pilate answered, "What I have written, I have written."

23 Then the soldiers, when they had crucified Jesus, took His garments and made four parts, to each soldier a part, and also the tunic. Now the tunic was without seam, woven from the top in one piece.

24 They said therefore among themselves, "Let us not tear it, but cast lots for it, whose it shall be," that the Scripture might be fulfilled which says: "They divided My garments among them, and for My clothing they cast lots." Therefore the soldiers did these things.

25 Now there stood by the cross of Jesus His mother, and His mother's sister, Mary the wife of Clopas, and Mary Magdalene.

26 When Jesus therefore saw His mother, and the disciple

whom He loved standing by, He said to His mother, "Woman, behold your son!"

27 Then He said to the disciple, "Behold your mother!" And from that hour that disciple took her to his own home.

28 After this, Jesus, knowing that all things were now accomplished, that the Scripture might be fulfilled, said, "I thirst!"

29 Now a vessel full of sour wine was sitting there; and they filled a sponge with sour wine, put it on hyssop, and put it to His mouth.

30 So when Jesus had received the sour wine, He said, "It is finished!" And bowing His head, He gave up His spirit.

31 Therefore, because it was the Preparation Day, that the bodies should not remain on the cross on the Sabbath (for that Sabbath was a high day), the Jews asked Pilate that their legs might be broken, and that they might be taken away.

32 Then the soldiers came and broke the legs of the first and of the other who was crucified with Him.

33 But when they came to Jesus and saw that He was already dead, they did not break His legs.

34 But one of the soldiers pierced His side with a spear, and immediately blood and water came out.

35 And he who has seen has testified, and his testimony is true; and he knows that he is telling the truth, so that you may believe.

36 For these things were done that the Scripture should be fulfilled, "Not one of His bones shall be broken."

37 And again another Scripture says, "They shall look on Him whom they pierced."

38 After this, Joseph of Arimathea, being a disciple of Jesus, but secretly, for fear of the Jews, asked Pilate that he might take away the body of Jesus; and Pilate gave him permission. So he came and took the body of Jesus.

39 And Nicodemus, who at first came to Jesus by night, also came, bringing a mixture of myrrh and aloes, about a hundred pounds.

40 Then they took the body of Jesus, and bound it in strips of linen with the spices, as the custom of the Jews is to bury.

41 Now in the place where He was crucified there was a garden, and in the garden a new tomb in which no one had yet been laid.

42. So there they laid Jesus, because of the Jews' Preparation Day, for the tomb was nearby.

John 20

1 On the first day of the week Mary Magdalene came to the tomb early, while it was still dark, and saw that the stone had been taken away from the tomb.

2 Then she ran and came to Simon Peter, and to the other disciple, whom Jesus loved, and said to them, "They have taken away the Lord out of the tomb, and we do not know where they have laid Him."

3 Peter therefore went out, and the other disciple, and were going to the tomb.

4 So they both ran together, and the other disciple outran Peter and came to the tomb first.

5 And he, stooping down and looking in, saw the linen cloths lying there; yet he did not go in.

6 Then Simon Peter came, following him, and went into the tomb; and he saw the linen cloths lying there,

7 and the handkerchief that had been around His head, not lying with the linen cloths, but folded together in a place by itself.

8 Then the other disciple, who came to the tomb first, went in also; and he saw and believed.

9 For as yet they did not know the Scripture, that He must rise again from the dead.

10 Then the disciples went away again to their own homes.

11 But Mary stood outside by the tomb weeping, and as she

wept she stooped down and looked into the tomb.

12 And she saw two angels in white sitting, one at the head and the other at the feet, where the body of Jesus had lain.

13 Then they said to her, "Woman, why are you weeping?" She said to them, "Because they have taken away my Lord, and I do not know where they have laid Him."

14 Now when she had said this, she turned around and saw Jesus standing there, and did not know that it was Jesus.

15 Jesus said to her, "Woman, why are you weeping? Whom are you seeking?" She, supposing Him to be the gardener, said to Him, "Sir, if You have carried Him away, tell me where You have laid Him, and I will take Him away."

16 Jesus said to her, "Mary!" She turned and said to Him, "Rabboni!" (which is to say, Teacher).

17 Jesus said to her, "Do not cling to Me, for I have not yet ascended to My Father; but go to My brethren and say to them, 'I am ascending to My Father and your Father, and to My God and your God.'"

18 Mary Magdalene came and told the disciples that she had seen the Lord, and that He had spoken these things to her.

95

19 Then, the same day at evening, being the first day of the week, when the doors were shut where the disciples were assembled, for fear of the Jews, Jesus came and stood in the midst, and said to them, "Peace be with you."

20 Now when He had said this, He showed them His hands and His side. Then the disciples were glad when they saw the Lord.

21 Then Jesus said to them again, "Peace to you! As the Father has sent Me, I also send you."

22 And when He had said this, He breathed on them, and said to them, "Receive the Holy Spirit.

23 "If you forgive the sins of any, they are forgiven them; if you retain the sins of any, they are retained."

24 But Thomas, called Didymus, one of the twelve, was not with them when Jesus came.

25 The other disciples therefore said to him, "We have seen

the Lord." But he said to them, "Unless I see in His hands the print of the nails, and put my finger into the print of the nails, and put my hand into His side, I will not believe."

26 And after eight days His disciples were again inside, and Thomas with them. Jesus came, the doors being shut, and stood in the midst, and said, "Peace to you!"

27 Then He said to Thomas, "Reach your finger here, and look at My hands; and reach your hand here, and put it into My side. Do not be unbelieving, but believing."

28 And Thomas answered and said to Him, "My Lord and my God!"

29 Jesus said to him, "Thomas, because you have seen Me, you have believed. Blessed are those who have not seen and yet have believed."

30 And truly Jesus did many other signs in the presence of His disciples, which are not written in this book;

31 but these are written that you may believe that Jesus is the Christ, the Son of God, and that believing you may have life in His name.

John 21

1 After these things Jesus showed Himself again to the disciples at the Sea of Tiberias, and in this way He showed Himself:

2 Simon Peter, Thomas called Didymus, Nathanael of Cana in Galilee, the sons of Zebedee, and two others of His disciples were together.

3 Simon Peter said to them, "I am going fishing." They said to him, "We are going with you also." They went out and immediately got into the boat, and that night they caught nothing.

4 But when the morning had now come, Jesus stood on the shore; yet the disciples did not know that it was Jesus.

5 Then Jesus said to them, "Children, have you any food?" They answered Him, "No."

6 And He said to them, "Cast the net on the right side of the boat, and you will find some." So they cast, and now they were not able to draw it in because of the multitude of fish.

7 Therefore that disciple whom Jesus loved said to Peter, "It is the Lord!" Now when Simon Peter heard that it was the Lord, he put on his outer garment (for he had removed it), and plunged into the sea.

8 But the other disciples came in the little boat (for they were not far from land, but about two hundred cubits), dragging the net with fish.

9 Then, as soon as they had come to land, they saw a fire of coals there, and fish laid on it, and bread.

10 Jesus said to them, "Bring some of the fish which you have just caught."

11 Simon Peter went up and dragged the net to land, full of large fish, one hundred and fifty-three; and although there were so many, the net was not broken.

97

12 Jesus said to them, "Come and eat breakfast." Yet none of the disciples dared ask Him, "Who are You?"— knowing that it was the Lord.

13 Jesus then came and took the bread and gave it to them, and likewise the fish.

14 This is now the third time Jesus showed Himself to His disciples after He was raised from the dead.

15 So when they had eaten breakfast, Jesus said to Simon Peter, "Simon, son of Jonah, do you love Me more than these?" He said to Him, "Yes, Lord; You know that I love You." He said to him, "Feed My lambs."

16 He said to him again a second time, "Simon, son of Jonah, do you love Me?" He said to Him, "Yes, Lord; You know that I love You." He said to him, "Tend My sheep."

17 He said to him the third time, "Simon, son of Jonah, do you love Me?" Peter was grieved because He said to him the third time, "Do you love Me?" And he said to Him,

"Lord, You know all things; You know that I love You."
Jesus said to him, "Feed My sheep.

18 "Most assuredly, I say to you, when you were younger, you
girded yourself and walked where you wished; but when
you are old, you will stretch out your hands, and another
will gird you and carry you where you do not wish."

19 This He spoke, signifying by what death he would glorify
God. And when He had spoken this, He said to him,
"Follow Me."

20 Then Peter, turning around, saw the disciple whom Jesus
loved following, who also had leaned on His breast at the
supper, and said, "Lord, who is the one who betrays You?"

21 Peter, seeing him, said to Jesus, "But Lord, what about
this man?"

22 Jesus said to him, "If I will that he remain till I come,
what is that to you? You follow Me."

23 Then this saying went out among the brethren that this
disciple would not die. Yet Jesus did not say to him that
he would not die, but, "If I will that he remain till I come,
what is that to you?"

24 This is the disciple who testifies of these things, and wrote
these things; and we know that his testimony is true.

25 And there are also many other things that Jesus did,
which if they were written one by one, I suppose that
even the world itself could not contain the books that
would be written. Amen.

Notes

Notes

Notes

Changing Hearts, Transforming Lives

❖ ❖ ❖ ❖ ❖ ❖ ❖

In 1970, Greg Laurie made a decision that would change his life forever: He decided to commit his life and future to Jesus Christ. From that point on, he began to share his experience with others. Now, twenty-five years later, Greg's passion to reach the world for Christ continues through Harvest Ministries, a non-profit organization to which Greg donates his time and talents.

Harvest Ministries exists for the sole purpose of presenting the life-changing message of Jesus Christ to as many people as possible and to help believers mature in their faith. Harvest Ministries coordinates the Harvest Crusades, public evangelistic events known for their informal atmosphere, contemporary music, and simple, straightforward messages presented by Greg. To date, over one million people have attended these nondenominational events since they began in 1990. Harvest Ministries also produces a quarterly newsletter, *Harvest Fields*, and ministry tools, as well as the "A New Beginning" radio and television broadcasts aired nationwide.

If you would like to know more about how Harvest Ministries can assist you and those dear to you, please write or call:

HARVEST
M I N I S T R I E S
GREG LAURIE

PO Box 4000 • Riverside • California • 92514-4000
1 • 800 • 821 • 3300